Praxis II Middle School Science (5440) Exam

"You never fail until you stop trying" - Albert Einstein

For inquiries;
info@xmprep.com

Unauthorised copying of any part of this test is illegal.

Praxis II Middle School Science (5440) Exam #1

Test Taking Tips

- ☐ Take a deep breath and relax
- ☐ Read directions carefully
- ☐ Read the questions thoroughly
- ☐ Make sure you understand what is being asked
- ☐ Go over all of the choices before you answer
- ☐ Paraphrase the question
- ☐ Eliminate the options you know are wrong
- ☐ Check your work
- ☐ Think positively and do your best

Table of Contents

SECTION 1 - GENERAL SCIENCE	
DIRECTION	1
PRACTICE TEST	2 - 40
ANSWER KEY	41
SECTION 2 - CELL BIOLOGY & PHYSIOLOGY	
DIRECTION	42
PRACTICE TEST	43 - 60
ANSWER KEY	61
SECTION 3 - EARTH & SPACE SCIENCE	
DIRECTION	62
PRACTICE TEST	63 - 93
ANSWER KEY	94
SECTION 4 - CHEMISTRY	
DIRECTION	95
PRACTICE TEST	96 - 117
ANSWER KEY	118
SECTION 5 - ECOLOGY & EVOLUTION & GENETICS	
DIRECTION	119
PRACTICE TEST	120 - 154
ANSWER KEY	155
SECTION 6 - PHYSICS	
DIRECTION	156
PRACTICE TEST	157 - 186
ANSWER KEY	187

Copyright © Educational Testing Group, All rights reserved.
This booklet may not be reproduced and transmitted in any form by any means without the permission of the publisher.
This booklet has been prepared and printed in USA.

TEST DIRECTION

DIRECTIONS

Read the questions carefully and then choose the ONE best answer to each question.

Be sure to allocate your time carefully so you are able to complete the entire test within the testing session. You may go back and review your answers at any time.

You may use any available space in your test booklet for scratch work.

Questions in this booklet are not actual test questions but they are the samples for commonly asked questions.

This test aims to cover all topics which may appear on the actual test. However some topics may not be covered.

Studying this booklet will be preparing you for the actual test. It will not guarantee improving your test score but it will help you pass your exam on the first attempt.

Some useful tips for answering multiple choice questions;

- Start with the questions that you can easily answer.

- Underline the keywords in the question.

- Be sure to read all the choices given.

- Watch for keywords such as NOT, always, only, all, never, completely.

- Do not forget to answer every question.

1

What does a hypothesis provide in a scientific investigation?

A) A scientific question that can be answered through existing literature
B) A summary of prior studies related to the investigation topic
C) An outline of the approach to be used in the investigation
D) A proposed explanation for the phenomena being studied

2

Before using a pH meter in measuring the pH of a water sample, what must a scientist do to ensure that the reading is accurate?

A) Warm the pH meter
B) Calibrate first the meter with a buffer solution.
C) Filter the sample to remove any organic matter.
D) Place the sample in a sealed container and refrigerate it.

3

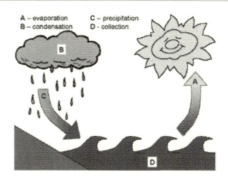

When does the condensation in the atmosphere occur?

A) After a rapid increase in the concentration of water vapor in the clouds
B) When there are microscopic particles in the atmosphere
C) When the relative humidity is slightly over 100 percent
D) When there are significant contrasts in temperature across the regions

Systematic error is a consistent and repeatable error associated with faulty equipment or a flawed experiment design.

Which of the following about systematic errors is not correct?

A) Incorrectly calibrated or incorrectly used measuring instruments are the main source of systematic errors.
B) Systematic errors lead to unpredictable fluctuations around the true value due to the problems with the calibration of the equipment.
C) If systematic errors are proportional to the true measurement, then it is called as Scale Factor Errors.
D) Random errors produce different values in random directions but systematic errors are consistently in the same direction.

Multiple strainmeters were set up on either side of an active strike-slip fault to determine how the bedrock deforms before minor earthquakes. The collected deformation data was correlated with seismograms for the area from the same period to help the scientists to learn if there are patterns in the deformation data that consistently precede minor earthquakes on the fault.

Which of the following is the dependent variable in the experiment given above?

A) Land surface's movement caused by minor earthquakes
B) Different seismic waves observed in minor earthquakes
C) Bedrock deformation before minor earthquakes
D) The intensity of the minor earthquakes for every fault activity

6

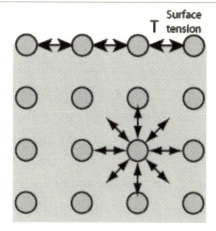

What type of bond is responsible for water tension and the formation of water drops?

A) Covalent bond
B) Ionic bond
C) Nuclear bond
D) Hydrogen bond

7

- It is the second most abundant element found in the Earth's crust.

- It has four electrons to share in chemical bonding, and thus can form long strings of atoms.

- It is used as a semiconductor of electricity.

Which of the following is the nonmetallic chemical element that is given above?

A) Carbon
B) Magnesium
C) Silicon
D) Hydrogen

8

The USGS installs seismographs near a dormant volcano to detect the increase in tremors that might indicate a coming eruption.

What other actions would be most useful in providing information for predicting an eruption of the volcano?

A) Surveying the vicinity of the volcano for a possible development of sinkholes.
B) Detecting any possible slight changes in elevation of the land surrounding the volcano through installing tiltmeters.
C) Keeping a record of the daily variations in the humidity of the air in the vicinity of the volcano.
D) Detecting any possible increase in acidity through monitoring the pH level of rainfall in the area.

9

A chart shows the amount of rain each month in a region.

What does the expression given above mean for a scientist?

A) Variables
B) Inferences
C) Data
D) Conclusions

10

A controlled experiment is a scientific test that is directly manipulated by a scientist.

Which of the following is a controlled experiment designed for?

A) Data
B) Hypothesis
C) Conclusion
D) Measurement

11

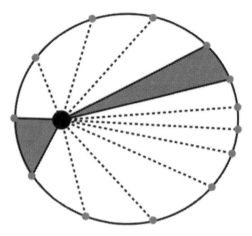

Which of the following is not one of Kepler's Laws of Planetary Motion?

A) All planets move about the Sun in elliptical orbits, having the Sun as one of the foci.
B) Planets move on elliptical orbits with the Sun at one focus.
C) An imaginary line drawn from the center of the sun to the center of the planet will sweep out equal areas in equal intervals of time.
D) The ratio of the squares of the periods of any two planets is equal to the ratio of the cubes of their average distances from the sun.

12

A researcher is analyzing a data collected for studying climate change.

In what way will the analysis become bias?

A) When the researcher notes the flaws in the research design that may have produced faulty data.
B) When the researcher removes data that significantly differ from expected results.
C) When the researcher alters the graphical presentation of the data set to make it clearer.
D) When the researcher summarizes the daily data in a weekly average.

13

Which of the following shows how a physical model that can be used to understand a complex natural system?

A) Dr. Murphy examines the rocks containing fossils to reconstruct the habitat of an extinct fossilized animal.
B) Dr. Lewis predicts winter weather for the next several years using historical data correlating sunspot cycles with short-term temperature changes.
C) Dr. Carter locates a deposit of oil and natural gases by measuring changes in the speed and direction of seismic waves produced by explosions or earthquakes.
D) Dr. Wenger made a scaled-down replica of San Francisco Bay to assess how a tsunami might affect the region.

14

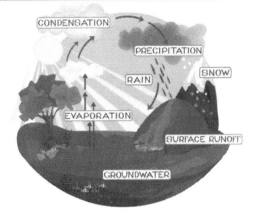

In the hydrologic cycle, water molecules absorb energy during which of the following process?

A) During the formation of ice from water
B) In the formation of a cloud from water vapor
C) The runoff along the land surface
D) The evaporation above the surface of the ocean

15

Dr. Morris suspects that the data he is collecting from an experiment may have a random error.

Which of the following is the best thing that Dr. Morris can do?

A) Identify any factors that could have caused the error and repeat the experiment to check the consistency of the data.
B) Show the results of the study to his expert colleagues to check for careless errors.
C) Change the hypothesis and begin the experimental process again adhering to the steps of the scientific method.
D) Recalibrate the instrument used in data measurement and perform the experiment once more.

16

The scientific method is a process for experimentation that is used to explore observations and answer questions.

Which of the following is the correct order of the steps in the scientific method?

A) Asking a question, making a hypothesis, testing the hypothesis, drawing conclusions and analyzing results.
B) Asking questions, making a hypothesis, testing the hypothesis, analyzing the results and drawing conclusions.
C) Making a hypothesis, testing the hypothesis, analyzing the results, asking a question and drawing conclusions.
D) Asking a question, analyzing results, making a hypothesis, testing the hypothesis and drawing conclusions.

17

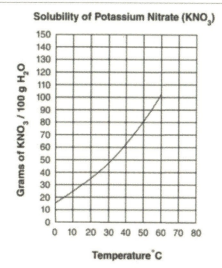

Approximately how many grams of Potassium Nitrate can be dissolved in 200 grams of water at 45°C?

A) 65
B) 70
C) 140
D) 160

18

In an **observational study** researchers simply collect data based on what is seen and heard and infer based on the data they collected.

Which of the following about an observational study is not correct?

A) The researcher has no control over the variables in an observational study.
B) There are no independent and dependent variables in an observational study.
C) In an observational study researchers always interfere with the subjects or variables.
D) Two things are important in an observational study; the variables are observed and the data is collected through observation.

19

A **controlled experiment** is a scientific test done under controlled conditions. Only one factor is changed at a time, while all others are kept constant.

Which of the following conclusion is true for a controlled experiment?

A) The conclusion must show that the data support the hypothesis.
B) The conclusion must show that the hypothesis was incorrect.
C) The conclusion must be reached for every experiment.
D) The conclusion must relate the data to the hypothesis.

20

Which of the following about the scientists is not correct?

A) Galileo Galilei is best known for describing the laws of planetary motion.
B) Sir Charles Lyell is best known for uniformitarianism, the idea that geological change is a prolonged process.
C) Edwin Hubble was an American astronomer who, in 1925, was the first to demonstrate the existence of other galaxies besides the Milky Way.
D) Nicolaus Copernicus was a Renaissance-era mathematician and astronomer who proposed the heliocentric solar system, in which the sun, rather than the earth, is the center of the solar system.

21

Which of the following is the description of loudness in an acoustic wave?

A) The rate of vibrations
B) The period of wavelengths
C) The magnitude of pressure variations
D) The number of cycles per second

22

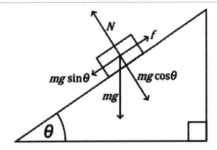

John wants to investigate the relationship between the effort needed to slide a given object along an inclined plane and the slope of the inclined plane.

What type of inclined planes should John use?

A) Those inclined planes that are made up of the same materials and the same length, but having different slopes.
B) Those inclined planes that have different lengths, but are made of the same material and having the same slope.
C) Those inclined planes of the same length, but having different slopes and made of different materials.
D) Those inclined planes that are made up of different materials but have the same slope and length.

23

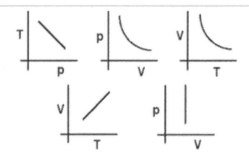

An **ideal gas** is a theoretical gas composed of many randomly moving point particles whose only interactions are perfectly elastic collisions.

For an ideal gas when all other conditions are constant which of the following variables are inversely proportional?

A) Pressure and temperature
B) Pressure and the number of moles
C) Pressure and volume
D) No two variables are inversely proportional

24

Mr. Fleming collects temperature data for the past 50 years from the Midwest. The data show a steady increase in daytime summer temperatures.

How can Mr. Fleming use these data to make predictions about how the average temperatures may increase in the following years?

A) Make a graphical presentation of the data, showing the line of best fit into the coming years.
B) Calculate the range of the data set and assume any future increases will be within that range.
C) Calculate the probable temperature for the coming year by adding the median of the data set and the average calculated temperature for each coming year.
D) Calculate the total change over time in the data set and use it in determining the minimum increase in the future.

25

Mr. Gregor is collecting data on the orientation of a limestone layer exposed along a highway to investigate the geologic history of a region.

What information should Mr. Gregor include in reporting the orientation of the limestone layer?

A) The depth at which the limestone was excavated
B) The angle at which the limestone was found
C) The degree of measurements showing the strike and dip of the bedding plane of the limestone
D) The changes in the dimensions of the limestone

26

Which of the following explains why water is capable of mechanical weathering?

A) It has a high surface tension
B) It has a very high capacity to store heat energy
C) It increases in density as it goes from 0 °C to 4°C and then decreases above 4°C
D) It increases in volume as it goes from a liquid to a solid state

27

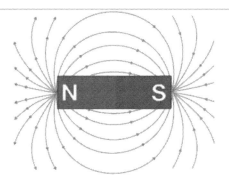

A bar magnet was placed at the bottom of a paper. The iron filings that were previously scattered onto the paper, became aligned along the magnetic field lines similar to that of the image above.

Which of the following causes this behavior of iron filings?

A) The magnetic field of the earth attracts the fillings.
B) The fillings are magnetized by the magnetic field.
C) The filings are repelled by the induced electric field.
D) The magnetic field ionizes the fillings.

28

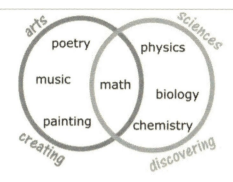

What is the primary reason why mathematics is assumed to be the language of science?

A) It has no cultural bias associated with its practice.
B) It describes predictable and testable relationships.
C) It reduces the uncertainty associated with chaotic systems.
D) It relies on the same processes as science.

29

$$2KNO_3 \rightarrow 2KNO_2 + O_2$$

How many moles of gaseous oxygen are released if six moles of potassium nitrate decomposes?

A) 5 moles
B) 4 moles
C) 3 moles
D) 2 moles

30

Which of the following steps is critical to do before using a pH meter to determine the pH of a water sample to ensure that the reading will be accurate?

A) The sample should be refrigerated in a sealed container.
B) The meter should be calibrated with a buffer solution.
C) The meter should be allowed to warm up.
D) The sample should be filtered to remove any organic matter.

31

Which of the following does an element's atomic number tell?

A) The number of electrons
B) The number of protons
C) Total number of protons and neutrons
D) Total number of electrons and protons

32.

A pond has become choked with weeds. To determine the actual dissolved oxygen content of the pond, a hydrologist is collecting water samples.

Which sample collection method should the hydrologist use to most closely reflect the actual dissolved oxygen content of the pond water?

A) Collecting water samples from below the pond's surface in various locations, filling and then sealing the containers rapidly and recording the locations.
B) Collecting water samples from the pond's surface near the outlet where the water is moving rapidly, and few weeds are growing.
C) Collecting the water sample from near the pond's inlet and avoid including any organisms or debris that may be in the water.
D) Collecting the water sample from near the bottom, making sure to leave some air space in the container and including some of the organic matter found in the pond.

33.

Which of the following will the scientist need, in addition to a balance and a ruler, to determine the magnitude of the unbalanced force acting on an object as it falls?

A) Digital timer
B) Steel protractor
C) Spring scale
D) 100mL graduated cylinder

34

Eutrophication is the process by which a body of water becomes enriched in dissolved nutrients (such as phosphates) that stimulate the growth of aquatic plant life usually resulting in the depletion of dissolved oxygen.

How is it possible to conclude that eutrophication of bodies of water has occurred?

A) By testing for the level of water acidity
B) By having greater species diversity in the water massive algae blooms
C) By having a vibrant, productive aquatic ecosystem
D) By having massive algae blooms

35

What must a scientist do to isolate the relationship between two variables in an experiment?

A) Make sure to experiment in a laboratory
B) Identify the scope of the investigation
C) Make sure to control the conditions that can alter the experiment
D) Make predictions of the full range of the experiment's possible outcomes

36

Which of the questions below would provide the best foundation for a climatologist's investigation of the causes of an extended drought in a region?

A) Why do droughts strike only in certain regions?
B) What variables affect the amount of precipitation received in the region during droughts?
C) How long is the average occurrence of droughts in other regions?
D) How could we manage the drought conditions in the region be best prevented?

37

Which of the following is not one of Kepler's Laws of Planetary Motion?

A) The moon passes through the earth's shadow
B) The moon passes through the sun's shadow
C) Earth passes through the moon's shadow
D) Earth passes through the sun's shadow

38

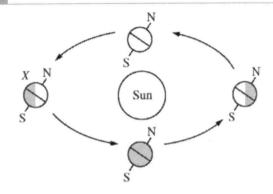

Earth's orbit around the Sun is given above. Which of the following is true of the Earth at location X?

A) The spring equinox occurs at X
B) The fall equinox occurs at X
C) The northern hemisphere experiences winter solstice
D) The northern hemisphere experiences summer solstice

39

In a closed electric circuit, which of the following copper wires has the smallest resistance?

A) Long wire with a large diameter
B) Long wire with a small diameter
C) Short wire with a large diameter
D) Short wire with a small diameter

40

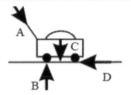

Which of the following vectors in the diagram represents the normal force?

A) A
B) B
C) C
D) D

41

Diamond is a solid form of carbon with a diamond cubic crystal structure. Because of which of the following is the diamond harder than graphite?

A) Its electron configuration is different
B) Its crystalline structure is different
C) It has a tetrahedral structure
D) None of these

42

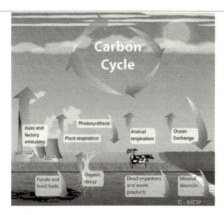

The carbon cycle occurs in the atmosphere, the hydrosphere, the biosphere, and the lithosphere.

Which of the following events describes one step in the movement of carbon from the atmosphere to the lithosphere?

A) Carbonic acid is produced from limestone during weathering.
B) Bicarbonate ions are extracted from seawater during coral reef formation.
C) Carbon dioxide is formed during the decay of biomass.
D) Atomic carbon is absorbed in seawater by deep-ocean sediments.

43

A scientific team collects data on twenty lakes in different regions of the US to study acid rain. A rain gauge is placed at each lake, and the amount and pH of precipitation that falls each week is recorded. At the same time, the scientists measure the pH of each lake's water and the slope of the ground within 100 meters of each lake's shore.

What is the dependent variable of this study?

A) The measured slope of the ground around each lake
B) The precipitation pH level
C) The amount of precipitation
D) The pH level of each lake's water

44

A deep well which is a confined aquifer has been contaminated with petroleum. To investigate the source of the petroleum contaminant, test wells were drilled in the north, east, south, and west areas near the well. The samples taken from the north and the east wells were found to be contaminated, while those from the south and the west wells were not.

It was concluded that the contaminant must be coming from the north and the east.

If the conclusion is not valid, which of the following can be the reason of it?

A) The samples were collected by different people.
B) The south and the west wells were drilled shallow above the confined aquifer.
C) The samples from the north and the south wells were collected when the well pump was off, while the other samples were collected when it was on.
D) The north and the east test wells are on the upgradient side of the original well where groundwater in the confined aquifer flows toward it.

45

Which of the following protects Earth from harmful charged particles coming from outer space?

A) Earth's magnetic field
B) Chemical reaction from gases
C) Ozone layer
D) Density of atmosphere

Which of the following scientific skills do you use when you see that the sky is cloudy?

A) Making observation
B) Drawing conclusion
C) Making inference
D) Posing a question

In astronomy, the most commonly used measures of distance are the light year, parsec and astronomical unit.

Which of the following is not a correct explanation?

A) A light-year is a distance that light can travel in one year in a vacuum (space).
B) One parsec is defined as the distance to a star that shifts by one arcsecond from one side of Earth's orbit to the other.
C) The astronomical unit (AU) is a unit of length, roughly the average distance from Earth to the Sun. Astronomical units are usually used to measure distances within our solar system.
D) Light years are usually used to measure distances within our solar system; Astronomical units are used to measure distances between the galaxies.

48

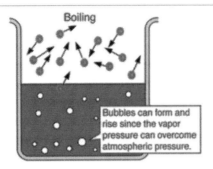

Which of the following about the vapor pressure of the liquid is true when a liquid is at its boiling point?

A) It is greater than the external pressure on the liquid.
B) It is equal to the external pressure on the liquid.
C) It is less than the external pressure on the liquid.
D) It can be either less or greater than the external pressure on the liquid.

49

Dr. Hover collects and tests the pH of water from six local ponds after significant rainstorms to determine whether rainfall increases the acidity of pond water.

What makes Dr. Hover's experiment design unreliable?

A) It does not have a clear hypothesis.
B) It has no manipulated variables.
C) It has no control data.
D) It has no dependent variables.

50

Suppose that a scientist proposes a hypothesis about how to develop vaccine for Corona virus.

Which of the following should other researchers do?

A) They should design new experiments to test the proposed hypothesis.
B) They should reject the hypothesis right away.
C) They should assume that the hypothesis is true.
D) They should change the hypothesis to fit their own findings.

51

Dr. Moore and his colleagues are analyzing the physical factors associated with the propagation of tsunamis.

Which of the following methods would be most useful and appropriate to use by Dr. Moore's team in conducting the study?

A) Examining the patterns produced when other types of waves are disrupted.
B) Creating underwater explosions using depth charges, and recording the waves produced in each explosion.
C) Producing waves under a wide range of different conditions using a large tank in the laboratory.
D) Examining how sea wells were formed using the historical records of large earthquakes.

52

Which of the following measures would be least likely affected by the limitation in the recording equipment which records air temperature higher than 100°F as being equal to 100°F?

A) Mode
B) Median
C) Range
D) Mean

53

Due to which of the following an enormous amount of energy is released in an atomic explosion?

A) The result of the conversion of chemical energy into nuclear energy
B) The result of the conversions of neutrons into protons
C) The result of the conversion of mechanical energy into nuclear energy
D) The result of the conversion of mass into energy

54

If an unbalanced force acts on an object, then the object will begin to accelerate.

Which of the following law explains this situation?

A) Kepler's Laws of Motion
B) Newton's First Law
C) Newton's Second Law
D) Newton's Third Law

55

A group of hydrologists wants to determine the average discharge of a particular river over the past 100 years using historical data.

What measure is best to use to determine the variability of this data set?

A) The median of the data set
B) The standard deviation of the dataset
C) The mode of the dataset
D) The arithmetic mean of the dataset

56

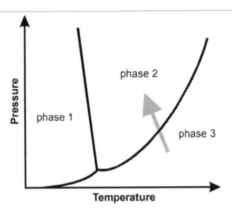

In the water phase-change above, which of the following processes is represented by the gray arrow?

A) Evaporation or the change from liquid to gas
B) Melting or the change from solid to liquid
C) Freezing or the change from liquid to solid
D) Condensation or the change from gas to liquid

57

Which of the following wave components is necessary to determine the distance of the earthquake from the station where primary and secondary seismic waves arrived?

A) Wavelengths
B) Arrival times
C) Frequencies
D) Horizontal or vertical displacements

58

Which of the following statements best describes the chemical makeup of a saltwater solution?

A) Uniform distribution of individual sodium and chloride ions among water molecules
B) Water molecules surrounding clusters of sodium and chloride crystals
C) Water molecules surrounding clusters of sodium chloride molecules
D) Uniform distribution of individual molecules of sodium chloride among the water molecules

59

In a polar covalent bond, the shared electrons are more attracted to one of the atoms than the other. The shared electrons are more likely to be near the atom whose electronegativity is higher.

Between which of the following elements the polarity of the covalent bonds would be greatest?

A) In the same column of the periodic table farthest from each other.
B) In the same row of the periodic table farthest from each other
C) In the same row of the periodic table adjacent to each other.
D) In the same column of the periodic table adjacent to each other.

60

Which of the following actions would most strongly bias the analysis of a researcher who is analyzing the data collected for a study of climate change?

A) Noting flaws in the research design that may have generated faulty data
B) Removing data that significantly differ from expected results
C) Altering the graphical presentation of the data set to make it more readable
D) Summarizing data collected on a daily basis into a weekly average

61

In the cycle of carbon in the earth's ecosystems, carbon dioxide is fixed by photosynthetic organisms to form organic nutrients and is ultimately restored to the inorganic state by respiration, protoplasmic decay, or combustion.

Which of the following is not true of the carbon cycle?

A) Carbon dioxide (CO_2) is fixed by glycosylation
B) 10% of all available carbon (C) is in the air
C) Plants fix carbon (C) in the form of glucose
D) Animals release carbon through respiration

62

Hydrologists use historical data to determine the average discharge of a particular river over the past 100 years to help establish the variability of the discharge of the river.

Which of the following is the best measure of the variability of this data set?

A) The median
B) The mode
C) The standard deviation
D) The arithmetic mean

A group of researchers is conducting a study about the behavior of animals that thrive in the hottest deserts of Africa to understand what these creatures need to survive in such a harsh climate. They are measuring how much they eat and drink per day as well as analyzing their activity during extremely hot temperatures.

As a generalization, which of the following is an application of the results of their study?

A) The results can only be applied to the environment where the researcher studied personally.
B) The results can be applied to similar environments, such as a desert climate in South America.
C) The results can be applied to the behavior of all animals, regardless of the climate they live in.
D) The results can't be applied to another area since generalization can only be used in qualitative studies.

In which of the following situations would professional scientific journals be most likely to reject an article for publication?

A) If an explanatory theory does not accompany the results
B) When the results contradict the findings of previous investigations
C) When the article lacks information about the methods used in the study
D) If the research is not based on the analysis of quantitative data

65

Which of the following questions would provide the best foundation for a climatologist who is investigating the causes of an extended drought in a particular region?

A) How long did other droughts in the region last?
B) What variables affect the region's precipitation during droughts?
C) How could the drought conditions in the region best be managed?
D) Why do droughts strike only in specific regions and not in others?

66

Which of the following scientific concepts was debunked by Einstein's Theory of Relativity?

A) Bohr's atomic model
B) Law of Conservation of Matter
C) Duality of Nature
D) Law of Inertia

67

What form of energy is stored in a battery in which the terminals are in contact with the rotating loops of wire that can be found in a turbine that uses wind power?

A) Mechanical energy
B) Chemical energy
C) Solar energy
D) Thermal energy

68

A scientist wants to determine the amount of carbon-14 in a sample of organic matter. Which of the following procedure would be the best way of this investigation?

A) A biologist establishing the metabolic rate of a cat
B) A botanist calculating the age of a living perennial herb
C) A paleontologist estimating when a dinosaur fossil formed
D) An archeologist ascertaining how long ago a fire pit was used

69

Which of the following is the most important thing a scientist should do to demonstrate to the scientific community that her discovery is legitimate?

A) Call for a press conference and announce her research.
B) Repeat the experiment in the presence of neutral observers.
C) Provide verifiable evidence to support her claim.
D) Explain the mechanism involved in her discovery.

70

Which of the following activities is the best example of the practice of science as an inquiry?

A) Determining which objects float upon placing different objects in a tank of water.
B) Identifying the materials needed to build a terrarium.
C) Determining how long a trip will take by assessing the road conditions.
D) Following directions in constructing an electric motor.

71

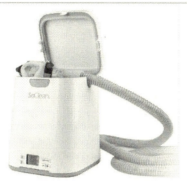

A Doctor wants to study the effectiveness of a CPAP Machines for sleep apnea. The Doctor records data on three groups of test subjects. The first group includes people who suffer from Apnea and are given the CPAP Machine. The second group includes people who suffer from apnea and are not given the CPAP Machine. The third group includes people who do not suffer from apnea and are given the experimental CPAP Machine.

Which of the following describes the research design for this study?

A) Observational study
B) Controlled experiment
C) Sample survey
D) None of the above

72

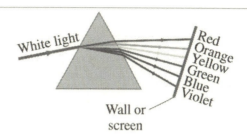

Which of the following phenomena is exhibited above when the white light passes through the prism?

A) Dispersion
B) Superposition
C) Diffusion
D) Reflection

73

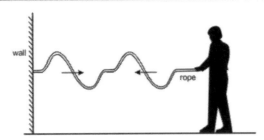

Based on the diagram given above that shows transverse wave along a rope, constructive interference of two waves will increase which of the following properties?

A) Frequency
B) Wavelength
C) Amplitude
D) Velocity

74

Upon gas expansion, which of the following phenomena is characterized by the inverse relationship between temperature and density?

A) Water vapor evaporation during hot days
B) Water vapor condensation during cool nights
C) Convection currents during warm days
D) Water vapor sublimation during cool dry days

75

• A dead tree decays.

• The top of a hill erodes slowly.

• A star uses up its nuclear fuel over years.

• A bottle of cologne is opened and the molecules spread throughout the room.

Which of the following scientific principles is illustrated in the four phenomena described above?

A) Physical balance called equilibrium
B) A reaction to something of a response
C) A state of disorder or entropy
D) A state of total confusion with no order called chaos

CONTINUE ▶

76

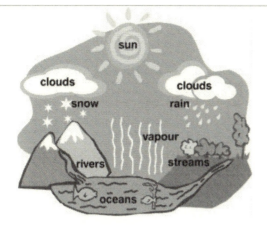

The water cycle is the cycle of processes by which water circulates between the earth's oceans, atmosphere, and land, involving precipitation as rain and snow, drainage in streams and rivers, and return to the atmosphere by evaporation and transpiration.

Which of the following about water cycle is not true?

A) Some part of the water is groundwater.
B) Water in the water cycle can exist only in liquid form.
C) The sun is the driving force of the water cycle.
D) Water is constantly moving from one place to another through the processes of evaporation, precipitation, transpiration, condensation, and runoff.

77

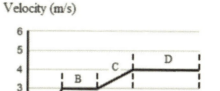
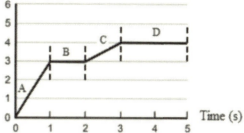

Based on the graph given above, in which time interval is the toy car's acceleration the greatest?

A) A
B) B
C) C
D) D

78

Which of the following is the best way for a scientist to make predictions about how the average temperatures in the Midwest may increase in the following years using the temperature data collected from the same area over the past 50 years?

A) Plot the data set and extend the line of best fit into the coming years.
B) Determine the range of the data set and assume any future increases will be within that range.
C) Take the median of the dataset and add that to the average temperature for each coming year.
D) Calculate the total change over time in the data set and assume it reflects the minimum increase in the future.

79

Which of the following is the independent variable in an experiment which measures the growth of bacteria at different temperatures?

A) Intensity of light
B) Temperature
C) The growth of the number of colonies
D) Type of the bacteria used

80

Some of the wave properties are defined below. Which of the following is not a correct explanation?

A) Wavelength is the distance between adjacent crests, measured in meters.
B) The period is the time it takes for one complete wave to pass a given point.
C) Frequency is the number of complete waves that pass a point in one second.
D) Amplitude is the height of the wave, in other words, it is the distance from the top of the crest to the bottom of the adjacent trough.

81

The **water cycle** describes how water evaporates from the surface of the earth, rises into the atmosphere, cools and condenses into rain or snow in clouds, and falls again to the surface as precipitation.

Which of the following terms is not associated with the water cycle?

A) Precipitation
B) Transpiration
C) Evaporation
D) Fixation

82

Scientists know that their results always contain errors because it is impossible to make an exact measurement.

Errors can be random or systematic. Which of the following about random error is not correct?

A) Random errors are random in nature but predictable and either constant or else proportional to the measurement.
B) Random errors are caused by unknown and unpredictable changes in the experiment.
C) The main reasons for random error are limitations of instruments, environmental factors, and slight variations in procedure.
D) Random errors often have a Gaussian normal distribution, and simple averaging out of various measurements can help offset them.

83

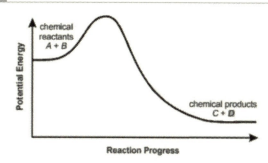

What is the indication of the higher potential energy of the reactants compared to the products?

A) As the products form, chemical energy will increase.
B) As the reactants combine, kinetic energy will decrease.
C) During the reaction, heat energy will be released.
D) During the reaction, heat energy will be absorbed.

84

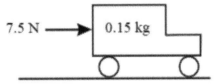

How many meter per second squared is the acceleration of the toy truck weighing 0.15 kg as it is being pushed with a constant force of 7.5 N?

A) 0.02
B) 50.0
C) 5.0
D) The toy truck's acceleration cannot be determined.

85

Which of the following best explains the reason why cellphones feel warm to touch as you recharge its battery?

A) Electric current in the wirings heat up surrounding molecules.
B) Charging the battery causes the formation of high-energy chemical bonds in the cell.
C) Electrical energy converted into chemical energy causes heat formation.
D) Electric current produces heat in the form of electromagnetic radiation.

86

Which of the following is used to test the effect of scent on a woman's mood by exposing her to a scent and observing her reactions?

A) Laboratory Observation
B) Naturalistic Observation
C) Experiment Observation
D) Two-Way Mirror Observation

87

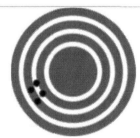

Which of the following will most directly affect the precision of the data the chemist collects in weighing the products of a chemical reaction?

A) The choice of weighing equipment to be used
B) The zeroing step on the scale before weighing
C) Establishing an average weight for the products through the use of repeated trials
D) The products' molecular weight reliance on accepted standard values

88

Which of the following is the most important thing a teacher can do to maintain a safe learning environment for the laboratory activity which covers pH determination?

A) Ensure that there are no electrical devices in the working areas

B) Make a list of students who are responsible enough to handle the chemicals

C) Review procedures for handling the chemicals being investigated

D) Review the reactions that occur between the chemicals being investigated

89

In the role of general public's support and appreciation of science, which of the following plays the most significant role?

A) Politicians who understand the value of expensive research projects that may have limited short-term benefits.

B) A business community aiming to improve competitiveness through funded research.

C) Schools providing topic and issues related to the science for broad understanding of students.

D) A university promoting the integration of pure research and applications of technology.

90. Which of the following strategies resulted in a biased interpretation of the findings of a scientific investigation?

A) Reviewing an abstract of the data analysis before submitting an article for publication in a journal.
B) Due to known procedural errors, flawed data collected during an extensive research project were rejected.
C) A scientist, lacking modern technological resources, formulates a hypothesis based on data collected.
D) Questioning the conclusions of the research due to the failure of including experimental data.

91.

Which of the following information is provided by the hypothesis during a scientific investigation?

A) A question that can be answered by researching existing literature
B) A format for outlining the approach to be used in the investigation
C) A summary of previous research on the topic being investigated
D) A proposed explanation for the phenomena being investigated

A researcher is investigating the geologic history of a region. Which of the following information would typically be included in the data he collects on the orientation of a limestone layer exposed along a highway?

A) The thickness of the limestone and how it has changed from its original horizontal position
B) The angle between an imaginary vertical line and the uppermost surface of the limestone
C) The degree measurements that show the strike and dip of the bedding plane of the limestone
D) The meters below the land surface of different sections of the top of the exposed part of the limestone

Reactants	Observation
• P and Q	Turns red after three hours
• Q and R	No change
• P and R	No change
• P, Q and R	Turns red after two minutes

The reactants P, Q, and R given above are colorless liquids.

Which of the following explanation is correct?

A) In the reaction of P and Q, R acts as a catalyst.
B) The combined product of Q and R reacts with P.
C) The combined product of P and Q reacts with R.
D) In the reaction between Q and R, P acts as a catalyst.

94

Human activities are partly responsible for changes in global temperatures experienced during the past 100 years.

Which of the following best explains why average global temperatures over the last 100 years is so high?

A) Natural systems do not generally shift that quickly unless disturbed by some external mechanism.
B) Natural systems are always changing, but generally at an almost constant rate.
C) Natural systems usually show randomly fluctuating rates of change over time.
D) Natural systems usually show decreasing rates of change as the system matures.

95

A pond has become choked with weeds and a hydrologist wants to determinate the dissolved oxygen content of the pond.

Which of the following methods should the hydrologist use to effectively collect water samples so that she will be able to find the dissolved oxygen content of the pond?

A) The water should be collected from below the pond's surface in various locations, filling and then sealing the containers rapidly and recording the locations.
B) The samples should be collected from the pond's surface near the outlet where the water is moving rapidly and few weeds are growing.
C) The water should be collected from near the bottom, making sure to leave some air space in the container and including some of the organic matter found in the pond.
D) The samples should be collected near the pond's inlet and should avoid including any organisms or debris that may be in the water.

96

A team of scientists sets up multiple strainmeters on either side of an active strike-slip fault to determine the deformation of the bedrock before minor earthquakes. This data is then correlated with seismograms for the same area. Both data sets were collected over a 20-year time frame, which will help the scientists determine if there are patterns in the deformation data that consistently precede minor earthquakes on the fault observed.

Given the information on the experiment, which of the following factors is the dependent variable?

A) The movement of the land surface during minor earthquakes
B) The types of seismic waves generated during minor earthquakes
C) The deformation of the bedrock prior to minor earthquakes
D) The frequency of fault activity resulting in minor earthquakes

97

Which of the following procedures would enable a soil scientist to adequately determine the volume of the air spaces in a soil sample in a metal container?

A) Comparison of volumes between the soil sample and a rock sample of the equal mass
B) Measuring the volume of water needed to saturate the soil sample.
C) Calculating the volume of the soil sample when it is spread out in a thin layer.
D) Observing the change in volume of the soil sample as it is compacted with a heavy object

An energy change that occurs as water evaporates from a pond on a warm day is best described by which of the following?

A) Water molecules move into the lower energy state due to the lower average kinetic energy of air compared to water.
B) The average kinetic energy of the water reduces as faster-moving water molecules break free from the water's surface.
C) The average kinetic energy of the overlying air decreases due to the adsorption of slower-moving water molecules on the surface.
D) The total kinetic energy of the air increases due to air molecules that pull water molecules into the gaseous phase.

What must scientists do to isolate the relationship between two variables in an experiment?

A) Experiment with a laboratory setting
B) Predict the full range of possible outcomes of the experiment
C) Control the conditions under which the experiment is carried out
D) Limit the scope of the experiment to the investigation of known facts

A high-yield drinking-water well draws water from a confined aquifer. A scientist wants to determine the source of the contaminant. In his investigation, he discovers that the test wells drilled to the north and east of the deep well were contaminated while the test wells drilled to the south and west were not.

The scientist then concludes that the contaminant must be coming from the north and east.

Which of the following factors would most likely reduce the validity of the scientist's conclusion?

A) The contaminated samples were collected on the same day by different people.
B) The contaminated test wells are on the upgradient side of the drinking water well where groundwater in the confined aquifer flows toward the well.
C) The uncontaminated samples were collected when the pump for the drinking water well was on, while the other samples were collected when it was off.
D) The uncontaminated test wells were drilled to a depth that is above the confined aquifer supplying water to the drinking water well.

SECTION 1 - GENERAL SCIENCE

#	Answer	Topic	Subtopic	#	Answer	Topic	Subtopic	#	Answer	Topic	Subtopic	#	Answer	Topic	Subtopic
1	D	TA	S1	26	D	TA	S2	51	C	TA	S1	76	B	TA	S2
2	B	TA	S1	27	B	TA	S2	52	B	TA	S1	77	A	TA	S2
3	B	TA	S2	28	B	TA	S1	53	D	TA	S2	78	A	TA	S1
4	B	TA	S1	29	C	TA	S2	54	C	TA	S2	79	B	TA	S1
5	C	TA	S1	30	B	TA	S1	55	D	TA	S1	80	D	TA	S2
6	D	TA	S2	31	B	TA	S2	56	D	TA	S2	81	D	TA	S2
7	C	TA	S2	32	A	TA	S1	57	B	TA	S2	82	A	TA	S1
8	B	TA	S1	33	A	TA	S1	58	A	TA	S2	83	C	TA	S2
9	C	TA	S1	34	D	TA	S1	59	B	TA	S2	84	B	TA	S2
10	B	TA	S1	35	C	TA	S1	60	B	TA	S1	85	C	TA	S2
11	B	TA	S2	36	B	TA	S1	61	A	TA	S2	86	A	TA	S1
12	B	TA	S1	37	A	TA	S2	62	C	TA	S1	87	A	TA	S1
13	D	TA	S1	38	A	TA	S2	63	B	TA	S2	88	C	TA	S1
14	D	TA	S2	39	C	TA	S2	64	C	TA	S1	89	C	TA	S1
15	A	TA	S1	40	B	TA	S2	65	B	TA	S1	90	D	TA	S1
16	B	TA	S1	41	B	TA	S2	66	B	TA	S2	91	D	TA	S1
17	C	TA	S1	42	B	TA	S2	67	B	TA	S2	92	C	TA	S1
18	C	TA	S1	43	D	TA	S1	68	D	TA	S2	93	A	TA	S2
19	D	TA	S1	44	B	TA	S1	69	C	TA	S1	94	A	TA	S1
20	A	TA	S2	45	A	TA	S2	70	A	TA	S1	95	A	TA	S1
21	C	TA	S2	46	A	TA	S1	71	B	TA	S1	96	C	TA	S1
22	A	TA	S1	47	D	TA	S2	72	A	TA	S2	97	B	TA	S1
23	C	TA	S2	48	B	TA	S2	73	C	TA	S2	98	B	TA	S2
24	A	TA	S1	49	C	TA	S1	74	C	TA	S2	99	C	TA	S1
25	C	TA	S1	50	A	TA	S1	75	C	TA	S2	100	D	TA	S1

Topics & Subtopics

Code	Description
SA1	Nature of Science
SA2	Physical Science

Code	Description
TA	General Science

CONTINUE ▶

TEST DIRECTION

DIRECTIONS

Read the questions carefully and then choose the ONE best answer to each question.

Be sure to allocate your time carefully so you are able to complete the entire test within the testing session. You may go back and review your answers at any time.

You may use any available space in your test booklet for scratch work.

Questions in this booklet are not actual test questions but they are the samples for commonly asked questions.

This test aims to cover all topics which may appear on the actual test. However some topics may not be covered.

Studying this booklet will be preparing you for the actual test. It will not guarantee improving your test score but it will help you pass your exam on the first attempt.

Some useful tips for answering multiple choice questions;

- Start with the questions that you can easily answer.

- Underline the keywords in the question.

- Be sure to read all the choices given.

- Watch for keywords such as NOT, always, only, all, never, completely.

- Do not forget to answer every question.

1

Reflex is a is an involuntary and nearly instantaneous response or a reaction to a stimulus.

Which of the following is not a characteristic of a reflex?

A) It is inborn.
B) It is acquired.
C) It is inherited.
D) It is automatic.

2

Peristalsis is a series of wave-like muscle contractions that moves food to different organs in the digestive tract.

Which of the following about peristalsis is not correct?

A) It is a muscular adaptation to move food through the digestive system
B) It is the continuous contractions that travel the whole length of the digestive organ.
C) It propels a ball of food through the esophagus, stomach, and intestines.
D) It is voluntary movements of the longitudinal and circular muscles, primarily in the digestive tract but occasionally in other hollow tubes of the body.

3

A description of the shape of a cell is called the cell morphology. The most common cell morphologies are cocci (spherical) and bacilli (rods).

What does the shape of a cell depend on?

A) It's function
B) It's size
C) It's structure
D) It's age

4

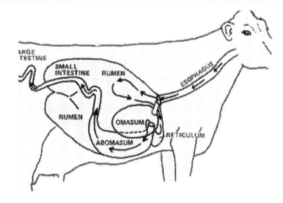

What is the primary function of dividing the digestive systems of ruminant animals into several different chambers?

A) To extract and meet daily water needs
B) To synthesize the required proteins from simple carbohydrates
C) To allow continuous feed of animal before digestion
D) To use microbial action to break down and extract nutrients from hard-to-digest substances such as cellulose

CONTINUE ▶

5

The cell is the basic structural, functional, and biological unit of all known organisms.

Which of the following about the cell is not correct?

A) Cell, in biology, is the basic membrane-bound unit that contains the fundamental molecules of life and of which all living things are composed.

B) Cell theory was proposed by Schleiden and Schwann. In 1839, Schwann and Schleiden suggested that cells were the basic unit of life.

C) The Cell Theory states: All living organisms are composed of cells. They may be unicellular or multicellular.

D) The term cell was coined by Schwann. He saw a series of walled boxes, reminded him of the cells of a monastery. What Schwann actually saw was the dead cell walls of plant cells.

6

Blood flows in two circuits in an arrangement called double circulation in most vertebrates, including humans.

What is the advantage of double circulation over a single circulation organization which is found in fish?

A) In double circulation, blood flow to different parts of the body can be regulated more precisely than in single circulation to meet localized oxygen needs.

B) In double circulation, the blood flows to the body tissues under higher pressure and faster, thus, allowing more efficient delivery of oxygen.

C) Oxygenated blood and deoxygenated blood can be mixed before passing through the tissues of the body.

D) There is a greater surface area in double circulation than in single circulation over which gas exchange between the blood and environment occurs, resulting in higher oxygen levels.

7

When a plant cell is placed in salty water, the cell loses water. What is the name of the movement of water?

A) Osmosis
B) Diffusion
C) Transpiration
D) Facilitated diffusion

8

Which of the following chemical processes generates the energy required for metabolic activities for most organisms?

A) Breaking down of glucose molecules
B) Breaking down of protein molecules
C) Synthesis of Glycogen molecules
D) Synthesis of Lipid molecules

9

An **anaerobic organism** is an organism that does not require oxygen for growth. There are three categories of anaerobes; obligate anaerobes (killed in the presence of oxygen), aerotolerant organisms (can live in oxygen or oxygen-free environments) and facultative anaerobes.

What is correct about facultative anaerobes?

A) They do not grow when oxygen is absent in their surrounding.
B) They do not grow when oxygen is present in their surrounding.
C) They can grow both with the presence and absence of oxygen.
D) They survive in harsh environmental conditions, provided there is oxygen available in their surrounding.

10

There are three distinct types of muscles in the human body; skeletal, cardiac, and smooth. Each type of muscle tissue has a unique structure and a specific role. Skeletal muscle moves bones and other structures, the Cardiac muscle contracts the heart to pump blood, the smooth muscle tissue forms organs like the stomach and changes shape to facilitate body functions.

Which of the following muscles in the human body function voluntarily?

A) Smooth
B) Cardiac
C) Sarcomere
D) Skeletal

11

Pollen is the male fertilizing agent of flowering plants, trees, grasses and weeds. It is also a major allergen that causes symptoms of seasonal allergic rhinitis

Which of the following part of the flower produces pollen?

A) Calyx
B) Anther
C) Stigma
D) Corolla

12

Which of the following is not a characteristic of the living things?

A) Living things move.
B) Living things are made of cells.
C) Living things obtain and use energy.
D) Living things grow and develop.

13

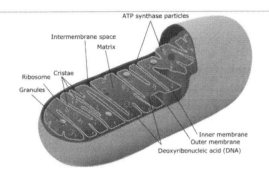

The **mitochondrion** is a double-membrane-bound organelle found in most eukaryotic cells.

Which of the following about the mitochondrion is not correct?

A) Prokaryotic cells are less structured than eukaryotic cells. Thus they contain fewer mitochondria compared to the eukaryotes.

B) Muscle cells contain a lot of mitochondria because they need more energy compared to other cells.

C) It is capable of using glucose and oxygen to produce energy. It produces large amounts of energy through oxidative phosphorylation of organic molecules during cellular respiration.

D) The cristae is the space formed by infoldings of the inner membrane. They expand the surface area of the inner mitochondrial membrane, enhancing its ability to produce ATP.

14

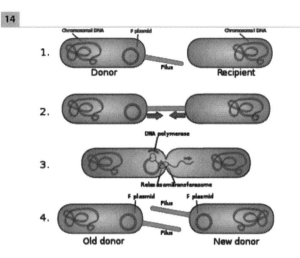

Conjugation is the process by which one bacterium (donor of the genetic material) transfers genetic material to another (recipient) through direct contact.

Why is the process of conjugation important in the bacterial life cycle?

A) Because it allows a bacterium to make an exact duplicate of itself.

B) Because it allows a bacterium to switch from being heterotrophic to autotrophic.

C) Because in many cases, conjugation serves to transfer plasmids that carry antibiotic resistance genes.

D) Because it allows deleterious mutations in the genome of a bacterium to be corrected.

15

Movement is powered by skeletal muscles, which are attached to the skeleton at various sites on bones. Muscles, bones, and joints provide the principal mechanics for movement, all coordinated by the nervous system.

Which of the following about the skeletal system is not correct?

A) Osteoporosis is a disease that causes bones to become weak and brittle.
B) A tendon is a fibrous connective tissue which attaches muscle to muscle.
C) Arthritis is a disorder of the joints. It involves inflammation of one or more joints.
D) Joints are structures where two bones are attached. A ligament is the fibrous connective tissue that connects bones to other bones.

16

If the population of bacteria in a culture flask doubles every 15 minutes, the population after 1 hour and 30 minutes will be how many times the population at the start?

A) 16
B) 32
C) 64
D) 128

17

Plant cell

Which of the following describes the distinct function of the central vacuole in plant cells?

A) It maintains hydrostatic pressure.
B) It strengthens the cell.
C) It stores energy-rich compounds produced in the cell.
D) It controls the movement of substances into and out of the cell.

18

Parts of the central nervous system (CNS) include all but not the following;

A) Venules
B) Brain
C) Axons
D) Spinal cord

19

Which of the following statements best summarizes the fundamental concept of the cell theory?

A) Each cell has its own DNA and RNA.
B) Living organisms are composed of one or more cells.
C) To maintain health, living organisms rely on specialized cells.
D) Cells break down of molecules to produce energy.

20

Skin is the natural outer layer of tissue that covers the body of a person or animal. The skin has three layers; epidermis, dermis, and hypodermis.

Which of the following is not a function of the skin?

A) Storage
B) Regulation of temperature
C) Protection
D) Sensation

21

Kingdom is a taxonomic rank that is composed of smaller groups.

Which kingdom is made up of organisms that have one cell with no nuclear membrane?

A) Monera
B) Protista
C) Fungi
D) Algae

22

What will happen if yeast cells have entirely used up the supply of oxygen that is present in their growth medium?

A) Production of ATP will stop, and yeast cells will die.
B) There will be an increase in carbon dioxide production, and the medium will become acidic.
C) NAD+ will be regenerated during the fermentation, and glycolysis will continue.
D) In the lysosomes of the yeast cells, there will be an accumulation of lactic acid.

CONTINUE ▶

23

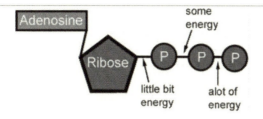

ATP (Adenosine triphosphate) is the principal molecule for storing and transferring energy in cells.

In which of the following stages ATP is generated most?

A) Chemiosmosis
B) Glycolysis
C) Fermentation
D) The Krebs cycle

24

Neurotransmitters are the brain chemicals that communicate information throughout our brain and body. They relay signals between neurons.

Which of the following is the most common neurotransmitter?

A) Epinephrine
B) Serotonin
C) Acetylcholine
D) Norepinephrine

25

The **microorganism** is an organism that can be seen only with the aid of a microscope and that typically consists of only a single cell.

Which of the following do microorganisms use to move?

A) Pili
B) Pseudopods
C) Flagella
D) Cilia

26

The highest level of organization for living things is the biosphere which encompasses all other levels.

The biological levels of organization of living things are arranged from the simplest to the most complex.

Cell: (1)   Tissue: (4)

Organelle: (2)   Organ: (5)

Organ System: (3) Organism: (6)

Which of the following identifies the correct sequence of the organization of living things?

A) (1) – (2) – (4) – (5) – (3) – (6)
B) (2) – (1) – (4) – (5) – (3) – (6)
C) (2) – (1) – (5) – (4) – (3) – (6)
D) (2) – (1) – (4) – (5) – (6) – (3)

CONTINUE ▶

27

Viruses adhere to the cell's surface by fitting specific parts of their surfaces to the surfaces of their host cells. This binding is called as "lock and key" model.

To determine which of the following is the "lock and key" arrangement between a virus and receptor sites on its host cells is most important?

A) Amount of time the virus remains infective outside the cell.
B) The rate of replication of virus inside the host cell.
C) The specific type of cell that is usually infected by the virus.
D) Amount of damage caused by the virus upon the host cell.

28

A series of wave-like contractions carry the food through the digestive tract. What is this process called?

A) Peristalsis
B) Absorption
C) Chyme
D) Digestion

29

Diffusion is a physical process that refers to the net movement of molecules from a region of high concentration to one of lower concentration.

Which of the following is necessary for diffusion to occur?

A) Carrier proteins
B) Enzyme and Energy
C) A concentration gradient
D) A semi-permeable cell membrane

30

Ribonucleic acid (RNA) occurs in different forms within organisms. It serves many different roles. There are different types of RNA.

In animal cells, which of the following is the primary role of the messenger RNA (mRNA)?

A) To serve as a template for the manufacture of new DNA strands within the cell nucleus.
B) To deliver amino acids to the ribosome.
C) To transfer the information needed from DNA to the ribosome.
D) To store long-term information.

31

Biological systems contain many types of regulatory circuits, both positive and negative. As in other contexts, positive and negative do not imply that the feedback causes good or bad effects.

Which of the following tends to slow down a process?

A) Negative feedback loop
B) Negative control molecule
C) Neurochemicals
D) Neurotransmitters

32

Facilitated diffusion is the process of spontaneous passive transport of molecules or ions across the cell membrane via specific integral proteins.

Which of the following about facilitated diffusion is correct?

A) It requires energy.
B) It is a kind of active transport.
C) It can only happen in plant cells.
D) A transport molecule is required to pass through the membrane.

33

Golgi Apparatus is a complex of vesicles and folded membranes within the cytoplasm of most eukaryotic cells. It is involved in secretion and intracellular transport.

What is the main function of Golgi Apparatus?

A) To break down proteins
B) To break down fats
C) To make carbohydrates
D) To sort, modify and package molecules

34

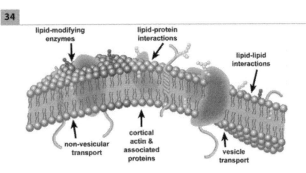

The cell membrane is a very thin membrane, composed of lipids and protein that surrounds the cytoplasm of a cell and controls the passage of substances into and out of the cell.

Which of the following is not true about the cell membrane?

A) It is made from phospholipids.
B) It controls the matter transport within the cell.
C) The cell membrane is the same as the cell wall in plants.
D) Both animal and plant cells have a cell membrane.

35

Which type of the cells evolved on the Earth first?

A) Heterotrophs
B) Eukaryotes
C) Autotrophs
D) Prokaryotes

36

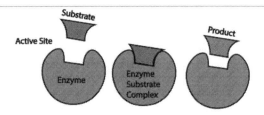

Enzymes are biological catalysts which speed up chemical reactions.

Which of the following is not true of enzymes?

A) They are made of proteins.
B) At high temperatures, they are deformed.
C) They work at a wide range of pH.
D) The enzyme is the lock and substrate is the key.

37

Photosynthesis takes place in two stages: light-dependent reactions and the Calvin cycle (light-independent reactions).

In which stage of photosynthesis is Oxygen given off?

A) Light reactions of photosynthesis
B) Krebs cycle
C) Reduction of NAD^+ to $NADH$
D) Dark reactions of photosynthesis

38

The membranes that make up the rough endoplasmic reticulum are composed of lipids just like the membrane that surrounds the entire cell itself. The surface of the rough endoplasmic reticulum is dotted with other organelles.

Which of the following is found on the rough endoplasmic reticulum?

A) Vacuoles
B) Ribosomes
C) Mitochondria
D) Microfilaments

39

Gap junctions directly connect the cytoplasm of two cells, which allows various molecules, ions, and electrical impulses to directly pass through a regulated gate between cells.

Which of the following is one of the primary functions of gap junctions between cell membranes?

A) Unifying the metabolic activity of a group of cells through permeable channels
B) Letting the exchange of genetic information between adjacent cells
C) Support the structural cohesion of cells that form a particular tissue
D) Letting surfaces of cells to contact the extracellular matrix

40

They are variably located on the back of the thyroid gland and humans usually have four of them.

Which of the following is explained above?

A) Thyroid glands
B) Parathyroid glands
C) Pineal glands
D) Pituitary glands

41

Amyloplasts are non-pigmented organelles found in some plant cells.

Which of the following is one of the functions of the "amyloplasts"?

A) They store starch in a plant cell.
B) They help in photosynthesis.
C) They store waste in animal cells.
D) They store yellow and green pigment.

CONTINUE ▶

42

Which of the following is not the function of the cardiovascular system in the human body?

A) To oxygenate the blood through gas exchange.
B) To transport nutrients, gases and waste products around the body.
C) To protect the body from infection and blood loss.
D) To help the body maintain constant body temperature (thermoregulation)

43

The simplest building block of a polymer is called as a monomer.

Which of the following are the monomers of polysaccharides?

A) Fatty acids
B) Amino acids
C) Polypeptides
D) Monosaccharides

44

In human beings, the homeostatic regulation of body temperature involves such mechanisms as sweating when the internal temperature becomes excessive and shivering to produce heat, as well as the generation of heat through metabolic processes when the internal temperature falls too low.

Which of the following is not included in homeostatic mechanisms in the body?

A) Respiration
B) Osmoregulation
C) Excretion
D) Thermoregulation

45

What is the best method to study the parts of the cells?

A) Using CAT scan
B) Using ultracentrifuge
C) Using a phase-contrast microscope
D) Using an electron microscope

46

Hormones, such as oestrogen and testosterone, are vital for the regulation of reproduction.

Which organ has the responsibility to release hormones for sexual maturity?

A) Thyroid gland
B) Hypothalamus
C) Pancreas
D) Pituitary gland

47

Mitochondria are rod-shaped organelles that convert oxygen and nutrients into adenosine triphosphate (ATP). The chloroplast is the organelle in a plant cell where photosynthesis happens.

Which of the following statements about mitochondria and chloroplast are not correct?

A) They both generate ATP.
B) They both produce energy.
C) They both have DNA and are capable of reproduction.
D) They both convert light energy into the chemical energy.

48

The cell membrane is a biological membrane that separates the interior of all cells from the outside environment. It consists of a lipid bilayer with embedded proteins.

Which of the following molecule is not found in the cell membrane of an animal cell?

A) Protein
B) Carbohydrate
C) Cellulose
D) Phospholipid

49

Which of the following is the largest of three fibers found in the cells?

A) Filaments
B) Microtubules
C) Microfilaments
D) Intermediate filaments

50

Which of the following statement best describes the part of a plant's root system where most cell divisions occur?

A) The region just beneath the protective cap of the cells at the root tip.
B) The outermost layer of the cells on the outside of root hairs.
C) The central column of the cells that runs the length of the root's interior.
D) The region between the root and the stem just below the ground surface.

51

Which is the correct statement regarding nerve signals?

A) Nerve signals travel on neurons whereas hormones go through the blood.
B) The nervous system maintains homeostasis whereas the endocrine system does not.
C) Endocrine glands produce neurotransmitters whereas nerves produce hormones.
D) The nervous system involves chemical transmission whereas the endocrine system does not.

52

Which of the following regulates the passage of ions and polar molecules in and out of a cell?

A) The attached carbohydrates to the membrane's outer surface.
B) The opening and closing of vacuoles adjacent to the membrane.
C) A selectively permeable cell membrane's phospholipid bilayer.
D) The diffusion gradient between the inside and outside of the membrane.

53

Skin is the soft outer tissue covering of vertebrates. It has three main functions; protection, regulation, and sensation.

Which of the following about skin is not defined correctly?

A) The epidermis is the thin, top layer of the skin that contains blood vessels, lymph vessels, hair follicles, and glands.
B) Sebum is an oily substance that is secreted by the sebaceous glands that help keep the skin and hair moisturized.
C) Collagen is is the most abundant protein in our bodies which gives our skin strength and elasticity.
D) Keratin is found in hair, horns, claws, hooves, and the outer layer of human skin which serves as a waterproofing protein in the skin.

54

Binary fission is the name of the process through which the bacteria commonly reproduce.

Which of the following gives the best definition of this process?

A) DNA from dead cells is absorbed into bacteria
B) DNA from one bacterium enters another
C) DNA doubles and the bacterial cell divides
D) Viral vectors carry DNA to new bacteria

55

Sex steroids, also known as gonadal steroids, are steroid hormones that interact with vertebrate androgen or estrogen receptors. Their effects are mediated by slow genomic mechanisms through nuclear receptors as well as by fast nongenomic mechanisms through membrane-associated receptors and signaling cascades.

Which of the following is not one of the three gonadal steroids?

A) Adrenocorticotropic hormone (ACTH)
B) Testosterone
C) Estrogen
D) Progesterone

The plasma membrane is a fluid combination of phospholipids, cholesterol, and proteins. The **viscosity** of the membrane can affect the rotation and diffusion of proteins and other bio-molecules within the membrane.

Which of the following determines the fluidity of the cell membrane?

A) Cholesterol
B) Glycolipid
C) Phospholipids
D) Carbohydrate chain

SECTION 2 - CELL BIOLOGY & PHYSIOLOGY

#	Answer	Topic	Subtopic	#	Answer	Topic	Subtopic	#	Answer	Topic	Subtopic	#	Answer	Topic	Subtopic
1	B	TA	S1	15	B	TA	S1	29	C	TA	S2	43	D	TA	S2
2	D	TA	S1	16	C	TA	S2	30	C	TA	S2	44	A	TA	S1
3	A	TA	S2	17	A	TA	S2	31	A	TA	S1	45	D	TA	S2
4	D	TA	S1	18	A	TA	S1	32	D	TA	S2	46	B	TA	S1
5	D	TA	S2	19	B	TA	S2	33	D	TA	S2	47	C	TA	S2
6	B	TA	S1	20	A	TA	S1	34	C	TA	S2	48	C	TA	S2
7	A	TA	S2	21	A	TA	S2	35	D	TA	S2	49	B	TA	S2
8	A	TA	S1	22	C	TA	S1	36	C	TA	S2	50	A	TA	S1
9	C	TA	S1	23	A	TA	S2	37	A	TA	S1	51	A	TA	S1
10	D	TA	S1	24	C	TA	S1	38	B	TA	S2	52	C	TA	S2
11	B	TA	S1	25	D	TA	S2	39	A	TA	S2	53	A	TA	S1
12	A	TA	S2	26	B	TA	S2	40	B	TA	S1	54	C	TA	S2
13	A	TA	S2	27	C	TA	S2	41	A	TA	S1	55	A	TA	S1
14	C	TA	S2	28	A	TA	S1	42	A	TA	S1	56	A	TA	S2

Topics & Subtopics

Code	Description
SA1	Physiology
SA2	Cells

Code	Description
TA	Cell Biology & Physiology

TEST DIRECTION

DIRECTIONS

Read the questions carefully and then choose the ONE best answer to each question.

Be sure to allocate your time carefully so you are able to complete the entire test within the testing session. You may go back and review your answers at any time.

You may use any available space in your test booklet for scratch work.

Questions in this booklet are not actual test questions but they are the samples for commonly asked questions.

This test aims to cover all topics which may appear on the actual test. However some topics may not be covered.

Studying this booklet will be preparing you for the actual test. It will not guarantee improving your test score but it will help you pass your exam on the first attempt.

Some useful tips for answering multiple choice questions;

- Start with the questions that you can easily answer.

- Underline the keywords in the question.

- Be sure to read all the choices given.

- Watch for keywords such as NOT, always, only, all, never, completely.

- Do not forget to answer every question.

1

Weathering is the breaking down of rocks, soil, and minerals as well as wood and artificial materials by the action of rainwater, extremes of temperature, and biological activity. There are three types of weathering, physical (mechanical), chemical and biological.

How does mechanical weathering differ from chemical weathering?

A) Mechanical weathering leaves the composition of the rock unchanged.
B) Mechanical weathering causes decomposition of rock through organic acids.
C) Mechanical weathering breaks down rock through hydrolysis.
D) Mechanical weathering changes rock through the process of oxidation.

2

In 1845, an area was surrounded by open fields. Today, the same area is swampy and surrounded by a forest.

Which of the following process is responsible for this change?

A) Conservation
B) Metamorphosis
C) Crustal movement
D) Ecological succession

A psychrometer is an instrument that uses the difference in readings between two thermometers, one having a wet bulb and the other having a dry bulb. It measures the moisture content of the air.

Which principle does a psychrometer is based on?

A) The relative humidity can be calculated by comparing the evaporative cooling that occurs in a particular location to the air temperature.
B) The apparent temperature can be identified by comparing the actual temperature in a location with the relative humidity.
C) The density of an air mass can be determined by calculating the molecular weight of dry air to the molecular weight of the actual air.
D) The adiabatic cooling of an air mass can be determined by comparing the actual pressure in a location to the theoretical sea-level pressure.

Why do overcast nights tend to be warmer than clear nights even when temperatures on a preceding day have been the same?

A) Because on overcast nights, the evaporation rates are substantially reduced
B) Because the clouds radiate infrared energy downward during overcast nights
C) Because the convection currents are unable to develop during overcast nights
D) Because on overcast nights, water vapor condenses and releases energy

When air rises it cools. As it gets colder, it cannot hold as much water vapor, eventually, the vapor condenses into clouds.

Which of the following processes leads to cloud formation when humid air rises over land?

A) Compression, warming to the dewpoint, and condensation
B) Compression, warming to the dewpoint, and evaporation
C) Expansion, cooling to the dewpoint, and condensation
D) Expansion, cooling to the dewpoint, and evaporation

6

Which of the following statements is true regarding temperature and pressure when you go deeper beneath the Earth's surface?

A) Both temperature and pressure increase
B) Both temperature and pressure decrease
C) Both temperature and pressure stay the same
D) Both temperature and pressure approach zero

7

What generally happens when a warm air and cold air converge at Earth's surface?

A) The sky becomes clear.
B) Wind movement drastically stops.
C) The clouds form slowly.
D) Stormy weather patterns develop.

8

Which of the following is a correct explanation about rocks and minerals?

A) Minerals are classified by their chemical composition and physical properties, while rocks are classified by their formation and the minerals they contain.
B) Traces of organic compounds may be found in minerals but not in rocks.
C) Mineraloids are both contained by rocks and minerals.
D) Minerals and rocks are both polymorphs.

9

Geologists use the Bowen's reaction series to explain the occurrence of various minerals in a particular igneous rock.

Which of the following events does it primarily define?

A) Different minerals in magma have different solidification temperature.
B) Crystals grow within a cooling magma at a particular rate.
C) There are different chemical changes that occur after a rock has solidified.
D) There are various crystal systems that will develop as a rock forms under pressure.

10

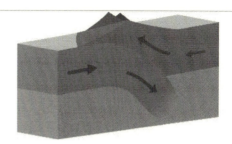

When two tectonic plates of different densities converge, which of the following features is formed?

A) A transform fault
B) An oceanic ridge
C) A transform fault
D) A deep-sea trench

11

The collision between a continental lithospheric plate and an oceanic lithospheric plate can lead to the formation of which of the following?

A) A mid-oceanic ridge
B) A chain of coastal volcanic mountains
C) A transform fault
D) A volcanic island

CONTINUE ▶

12

Which of the following geologic events caused the formation of the Atlantic Ocean?

A) The erosion of a plate margin caused by repeated continental glaciations
B) The subduction of one continental plate beneath another
C) The development of a large syncline east of the Appalachian Mountains
D) The growth of a rift valley along a primary fracture zone in the crust

13

Alfred Wegener was the first to propose the theory of continental drift in which he explained that continents had changed position over time. However, many scientists rejected his approach despite having some compelling evidence of his claim.

What was the primary scientific reason causing many geologists to reject Wegener's continental drift proposal?

A) He was considered an amateur who was trained in a different scientific discipline.
B) His hypothesis lacked a convincing mechanism to explain what forces moved the continents.
C) He believed his evidence was strong; hence he did not argue the merits of his ideas.
D) His fieldwork lacked the rigor associated with most sciences of the day.

14

Which of the following best helps to explain why some localities have normally great tidal ranges (up to 60 feet) and others have one- to two-foot tidal ranges?

A) The relative positions of the Moon and Sun are different at different localities.
B) The Coriolis effect and rotation of the Earth tend to enhance tidal bow in the higher latitudes.
C) Ocean floor topography and the shape of the coastline serve to amplify tidal bow at specific localities.
D) Tradewinds push the water into large tidal bulges near rocky shorelines.

15

The winds at the Earth's surface typically flow across the isobars that separate a high-pressure center from a low-pressure center, while the wind flow aloft is typically parallel to atmospheric pressure isobars.

What is most likely causing the difference between wind flow aloft and at the Earth's surface?

A) The increased frictional drag on wind flow at the surface of the Earth
B) The reduced strength of the Coriolis effect on wind flow aloft
C) The greater divergence of winds above a low-pressure system
D) The decreased atmospheric pressure with increased altitude

16

What contributes most of the dissolved salts in the Earth's oceans?

A) The marine biological activities
B) The atmospheric deposition
C) The weathering of continental rocks
D) The eruptions of hotspot volcanoes under the oceans

17

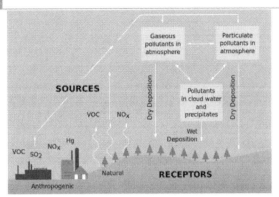

Which of the following can effectively reduce acid precipitation from power plant emissions?

A) Using lime and water in exhausts to react sulfur dioxide with calcium hydroxide
B) Using mesh filtration systems to filter dust particles generated by the breakdown of coal
C) Using smokestack catalytic converters to convert carbon monoxide to carbon dioxide
D) Removing volatile hydrocarbon compounds found in coal before burning the fuel

18

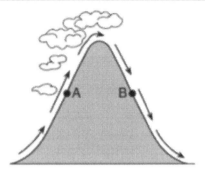

According to the image given above, which of the following comparison about air temperature and humidity at points A & B is correct?

A) B is cooler and drier than A
B) B is cooler and wetter than A
C) B is warmer and wetter than A
D) B is warmer and drier than A

19

The Brazilian Current in the Southern Hemisphere moves toward the South Pole, while the Gulf Stream in the Northern Hemisphere moves toward the North Pole.

What effect will this pole-ward movement bring to the coastal areas bordering these currents when compared to the inland areas at the same latitude?

A) The coastal areas will be warmer than the inland areas.
B) The coastal areas will be more arid than the inland areas.
C) The coastal areas will have more advection fogs than the inland areas.
D) The coastal areas will have shorter growing seasons than the inland areas.

20

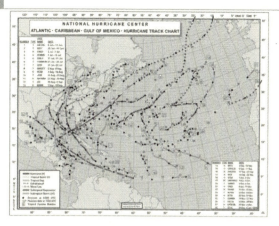

Which phenomenon primarily causes the formation of Atlantic hurricanes between June and November?

A) The subtropical jet stream's position during these months
B) An increased activity of the northeast trade winds during these months
C) The average sea surface temperature in the Atlantic during these months
D) The northward shift of the inter-tropical convergence zone during these months

21

By volume, dry air contains 78.09% nitrogen, 0.93% argon, 0.04% carbon dioxide, and small amounts of other gases. Air also contains a variable amount of water vapor, on average around 1% at sea level, and 0.4% over the entire atmosphere.

What is the average concentration of oxygen in the ambient air?

A) 10.95%
B) 20.95%
C) 25.95%
D) 30.95%

22

Nitrogen is the chemical element with the symbol N. It was first discovered by Scottish physician Daniel Rutherford in 1772. It is a colourless, odourless, tasteless gas in Earth's atmosphere and is a constituent of all living matter.

What is the approximate percentage of nitrogen in the air at sea level?

A) 5%
B) 10%
C) 20%
D) 78%

23

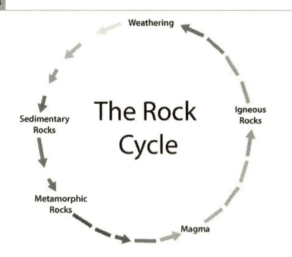

The rock cycle describes the time-consuming transitions through geologic time among the three main rock types: sedimentary, metamorphic, and igneous.

Which of the following statements about the formation of rocks is best supported by the rock cycle?

A) Metamorphic rock must melt before it changes to sedimentary rock.
B) Magma must be weathered before it changes to metamorphic rock.
C) Sedimentary rock must melt before it changes to metamorphic rock.
D) Sediment must be compacted and cemented before it changes to sedimentary rock.

24

Which of the following gases are believed to contribute most to global warming when they are released into the atmosphere?

A) Carbon dioxide and nitrogen
B) Carbon dioxide and methane
C) Carbon monoxide and methane
D) Carbon monoxide and nitrogen monoxide

25

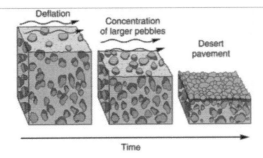

Desert pavement phenomenon happens when a thin layer of closely packed pebbles and cobbles covers the ground surface.

What is the primary cause of this phenomenon?

A) The differential erosion of sediments by wind
B) The slow dispersal of material from the base of alluvial fans by gravity
C) The breakup of bedrock under hot and dry conditions
D) The deposition of coarse-grained sediments during flash flooding

26

Air is the mixture of gases that forms the Earth's atmosphere and that we breathe.

Which of the following is the major gas in the air?

A) Oxygen
B) Nitrogen
C) Hydrogen
D) Carbon dioxide

27

Computer models are used to investigate possible consequences of increased average global temperatures on various Earth systems.

Based on these models, which change is likely to occur in the Earth's systems that are mostly associated with an increase in average global temperatures?

A) There will be long periods without adequate rainfall, resulting in some regions' experiencing drier droughts.
B) There will be rapid changes in weather conditions as a result of an increased frequency of jet stream winds' position shifting.
C) Coriolis effect will be stronger, causing a reduced occurrence of hurricanes in tropical areas.
D) Anomalous weather conditions such as El Niño will occur at longer intervals.

28

How do water vapor and carbon dioxide affect the radiation emitted by the Sun and Earth?

A) Carbon dioxide and water vapor absorb ultraviolet radiation emitted by the Sun, and they transmit it as an infrared radiation from Earth's surface into the upper atmosphere.
B) Carbon dioxide and water vapor absorb much of the ultraviolet radiation from the sun, and they transmit it as a visible light reflected from Earth's surface.
C) Carbon dioxide and water vapor absorb the infrared radiation released by the Sun, and they trap it as an ultraviolet radiation in the lower atmosphere of the Earth.
D) Carbon dioxide and water vapor allow much of the Sun's radiation to reach Earth's surface, but they absorb much of the infrared radiation emitted by Earth.

29

The presence of a layer of conglomerate in bedrock just above a layer of shale is consistent with the sequences of events involving which of the following?

A) Cooling and hardening of lava over a layer of rock from a volcanic eruption
B) Lowering the water level of a large lake, which eventually formed into a beach
C) Accumulation of shells developed from one-celled organisms
D) Localized recrystallization of shale from mud deposits

30

Coriolis effect is an effect whereby a mass moving in a rotating system experiences a force acting perpendicular to the direction of motion and to the axis of rotation.

What happens to the wind currents as influenced by the Coriolis effect?

A) The wind currents tend to cool off as they converge and rise
B) The wind flows in a straight path as it crosses lines of longitude
C) The wind currents diverge and sink, and eventually heat up
D) The wind currents tend to curve as they flow over Earth's surface

31

What causes the colorful displays in the atmosphere called the aurora borealis?

A) The nuclear disintegration of radioactive isotopes in the thermosphere
B) The combustion of dust particles in the stratosphere
C) The chemical reaction of molecules in the troposphere
D) The interaction of the solar wind and the magnetosphere, causing excitation of gases

32

Which of the following has provided the most information about the structure of Earth's core, mantle, and lower crust?

A) Analysis of Active Lava Flows
B) Collection of samples from deep boreholes drilled into Earth
C) Measurement of the intensity and fluctuations of Earth's magnetic field
D) Studies of the speeds and travel paths of seismic waves passing through Earth

33

Minerals such as gold, platinum, and native copper are formed in concentrated placer deposits in alluvial sands and gravels.

Which of the following explains this formation?

A) These materials are formed because they are resistant to chemical weathering than the surrounding matrix.
B) These minerals are formed because they have smaller grains than most other minerals.
C) These minerals resist displacement by moving water.
D) These materials are deposited quickly when stream velocity decreases due to their higher gravity properties.

34

A particulate matter (PM), also known as particle pollution, is an atmospheric pollutant. What comprises a particulate matter?

A) Gases and acidic liquids
B) Small fragments of natural substances visible to the unaided eye
C) Solid materials and droplets which are small enough to be suspended in the air
D) Chemicals that trap heat and absorb infrared energy

35

What causes the air moving from the poles toward the equator to turn westward?

A) The size and shape of land masses near the path of the wind
B) The larger cities surrounded by farmlands
C) The sudden changes in the magnetic field of the Earth
D) The rotation of the Earth

CONTINUE ▶

36

Which statement below illustrates a scientific inference?

A) Based on the data, Mars once had liquid water.
B) Gathering repeated measurements will reduce random error.
C) Proper handling of electrical equipment involves putting a ground wire.
D) There are three significant figures in a certain measurement.

37

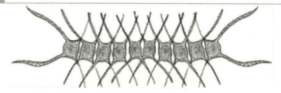

Phytoplanktons are single-celled organisms which are similar to terrestrial plants in that they contain chlorophyll and require sunlight in order to live and grow.

How does a phytoplankton help in balancing the Earth's climate?

A) It takes in ozone and produces diatomic oxygen.
B) It absorbs carbon dioxide and produces oxygen.
C) It uses nitrogen oxides and produces methane.
D) It takes in water vapor and produces carbon dioxide.

38

What was the primary cause of the changes to the Earth's climate system, causing the 1991 eruption of Mount Pinatubo in the Philippines?

A) The accumulation of sulfur dioxide in the lower stratosphere
B) The accumulation of some particulates that were trapped in the upper troposphere
C) The accumulation of carbon dioxide in the upper stratosphere
D) The accumulation of nitrogen oxide that increased smog in the lower troposphere

39

The moon is an astronomical body that orbits the Earth, making it the only permanent natural satellite the Earth has.

How much smaller is the moon as compared to the Earth?

A) The moon and the Earth are of the same size.
B) The moon is about one half the size of the Earth.
C) The moon is about one fourth the size of the Earth.
D) The moon is about one eighth the size of the Earth.

40

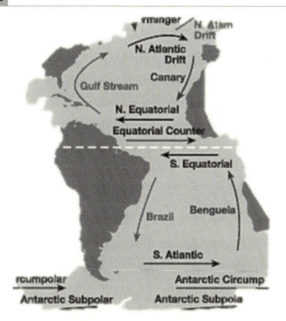

What is the primary effect of Coriolis force on ocean surface currents?

A) It causes the currents to curve from a straight path.
B) It causes the currents to expand as they enter cool waters.
C) It increases the friction between currents and ocean floor.
D) It decreases the speed of the currents relative to adjacent ocean waters or land masses.

41

The Earth atmosphere is composed of many gases that are vital for the survival of all living organisms.

Which of the following pairs of gases lists the two most abundant gases in the Earth's atmosphere?

A) Carbon dioxide and oxygen
B) Carbon dioxide and nitrogen
C) Nitrogen and oxygen
D) Nitrogen and hydrogen

42

Why does the sky appear blue?

A) Because the air molecules selectively scatter the shorter wavelengths of visible light
B) Because the air molecules reflect the longer wavelengths of visible light
C) Because the water vapor refracts visible light into its component frequencies
D) Because the water vapor selectively absorbs visible light at particular wavelengths

43

In predicting whether the skies will change from clear to cloudy, which of the following would give the most useful information?

A) Relative humidity
B) Temperature
C) Barometric pressure
D) Wind speed

44

This landform is an area of highland that has a relatively flat terrain at its surface. It is elevated significantly compared to its surroundings and is also known by other names such as high plain or tableland.

Which of the following is another name given to landform?

A) Lowland
B) Mountain System
C) Coastal Plain
D) Plateau

45

Which of the following condition must be present for a low-pressure system to continue to develop into a stronger low-pressure system?

A) The divergent wind flow occurring at the base of the low-pressure system
B) The cold-air advection occurring above the low- pressure system
C) The convection of relatively warm air within the low-pressure system
D) The convergent wind flow occurring above the low-pressure system

46

Which element comprises the most significant amount of rocks and minerals?

A) Carbon (C)
B) Aluminum (Al)
C) Hydrogen (H)
D) Silicon (Si)

47

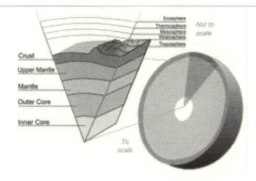

Which of the following can identify the structure of the Earth's core, mantle, and lower crust best?

A) Measuring the intensity and fluctuations of Earth's magnetic field
B) Examining the properties of lava
C) Collecting samples from deep boreholes drilled into Earth
D) Studying the speeds and travel paths of seismic waves passing through Earth

48

Fog is a cloudlike layer of water droplets or ice crystals near the surface of the earth which reduces the visibility.

When is an advection fog most likely to occur?

A) A layer of warmer air traps a cold air beneath it.
B) A hot dry air in the surface cools after sunset.
C) A cool moist air warms as it flows down a mountainside.
D) A warm moist air flows over cold ocean water.

49

Which of the following explains the presence of the Earth's core which is composed of iron and nickel?

A) The heavier elements are pulled toward the core by the intense gravitational field at the center of Earth.
B) Earth was originally formed as a solid which eventually melted, and the denser iron and nickel sank down through the less dense layers of silicate material to the center.
C) The ancient Earth was initially composed of iron and nickel, and the rest of the planet was added later by accretion.
D) The Earth's magnetic field pulls molten iron and nickel toward the center, leaving nonmagnetic silicates behind.

50

Onshore and offshore winds occur over the areas where land masses meet large bodies of water.

Which of the following is the reason why onshore and offshore winds occur?

A) Water has a higher specific heat than land
B) The land has a higher specific heat than water
C) The land absorbs more thermal energy
D) Water cannot absorb as much thermal energy as the land

51

The temperature of the air nearest the ground surface often drops as sunlight strikes damp ground shortly after sunrise.

Which of the following best explains this early morning cooling of the air?

A) The condensation of water from water vapor
B) The sublimation of water vapor from the ground surface
C) The phase change of water from liquid to gas
D) The sensible heat decreases as the humidity near the ground surface increases

52

How do lichens, plant roots, and fungi are able to weather rock chemically?

A) By drawing molecular water from the crystals that make up the rock
B) By producing acids that cause the decomposition of the rock
C) By extracting minerals directly from the rock through osmosis
D) By manufacturing salts that alter the rock's crystal structure

53

Which geologic materials cannot typically withstand shaking caused by a major earthquake?

A) Materials made up of heavily fractured shale
B) Materials made up of karstic limestone
C) The unconsolidated silt and clay materials
D) The massive granite materials

54

What causes the variations in tidal ranges across some localities?

A) The difference between the relative positions of the Moon and the Sun from the Earth
B) The Coriolis effect and rotation of the Earth on its axis
C) The ocean floor topography and the coastline shapes
D) The winds' direction

55

Freshwater accounts for approximately 3% of the water on Earth. In which area freshwater is most likely be found?

A) Groundwater
B) In the atmosphere
C) Lakes and ponds
D) Glaciers and ice caps

56

Upwelling is an oceanographic phenomenon in which deep, cold water rises toward the surface.

What is the primary reason of the upwelling of cold water in the large sections of the west coasts of North and South America?

A) Due to prevailing wind patterns, water moves away from the coast.
B) The steep offshore topography that forces deep water currents upward.
C) Solar heating that caused rapid evaporation of surface water.
D) The respiration of microorganisms that caused the reduction in density of deep-ocean water.

57

Tides are the rise and fall of sea levels caused by the combined effects of the gravitational forces exerted by the Moon and the Sun and the rotation of Earth.

Which of the following is the main cause of the existence of tides?

A) Water moves due to the Earth's rotation on its axis.
B) Strong winds blow water onto the coasts causing tides.
C) Tides are caused by the differences in how much the sun pulls on different parts of the Earth.
D) Tides are caused by the differences in how much the moon pulls on different parts of the Earth.

58

What is the primary reason why lunar eclipses occur much less frequently than the days moon orbits Earth?

A) The plane of the moon's orbit around Earth is tilted relative to the plane of Earth's orbit around the sun.
B) The tilt of Earth's axis relative to the sun changes regularly as Earth orbits the sun.
C) The distance from Earth to the sun is greater than the distance from Earth to the moon.
D) The speed of Earth's orbit around the sun is greater than the moon's orbital speed around Earth.

59

Which of the following are the rocks formed from previously existing rocks that have been modified by temperature, pressure, and mechanical stress?

A) Basaltic rocks
B) Igneous rocks
C) Metamorphic rocks
D) Sedimentary rocks

60

The oxygen in our atmosphere is essential for life. The atmosphere blocks some of the Sun's dangerous rays from reaching Earth and makes Earth livable. It traps heat, making Earth a comfortable temperature.

Which of the following statements is not true about the atmosphere?

A) It is the layer in which weather occurs.
B) It is the layer that contains the ozone layer.
C) It is the layer of gases that surrounds the Earth.
D) It is the layer with a uniform temperature and pressure.

61

Which of the following shows the correct order of the layers of Earth's atmosphere from Earth to space?

A) Troposphere, stratosphere, mesosphere, thermosphere
B) Stratosphere, troposphere, mesosphere, thermosphere
C) Mesosphere, troposphere, stratosphere, thermosphere
D) Thermosphere, troposphere, stratosphere, mesosphere

Which of the following can be accounted for the soil formation in mountainous regions?

A) The erosion and sediment deposition
B) The gradual movement of tectonic plates
C) The mechanical and chemical rock weathering
D) The decomposition through fungi and bacteria

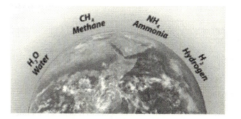

Ozone layer absorbs most of the ultraviolet radiation reaching the earth from the sun.

Which of the following about the ozone layer is not correct?

A) In the 1970s, people all over the world started realizing that the ozone layer was getting thinner.
B) Chemicals called chlorofluorocarbons (CFCs) are a reason we have a thinning ozone layer.
C) The ozone layer, sunscreen of our Earth's, absorbs about 100 percent of devastating UV light.
D) Ozone molecules, which are simply made of three joined oxygen atoms, are always being destroyed and reformed naturally.

64

Which of the following important consequences for the soil in desert and grassland ecosystems is caused by an irrigation used over a long period of time?

A) Natural soil micro-organisms were depleted
B) Upper soil horizons accumulate salts
C) Erosion and consequent loss of topsoil
D) Fungal pathogens below the soil surface increases

65

Climate is defined as the weather conditions that are characteristic of an area in general or over a long period.

What are the two main factors that determine the climate of a region?

A) Temperature and precipitation
B) Pressure and temperature
C) Altitude and pressure
D) Altitude and temperature

66

A galaxy is a gravitationally bound system of stars, stellar remnants, interstellar gasses, dust, and dark matter. Recent estimates made by astronomers say that there are more than a billion galaxies in the observable universe and they are usually categorized based on their shape.

Which of the following shape is taken by our galaxy, the Milky Way?

A) Spiral Galaxy
B) Cloud Galaxy
C) Elliptical Galaxy
D) Irregular Galaxy

67

Which of the following is the primary factor responsible for the variability in average annual temperatures in Arizona?

A) The range in elevation in different parts of the state
B) The extreme changes in wind direction that occur over the course of the year
C) The extent of the rain shadows that exist on the leeward sides of some mountains
D) The intense radiational cooling that occurs in some locations in the state

CONTINUE ▶

68

The idea of continental drift, developed by Alfred Wegener in 1912, has been subsumed by the theory of plate tectonics, which explains how the continents move.

Which of the following pieces of evidence was used by Alfred Wegener to validate his Theory of Continental Drift?

A) Larger fault lines due to earthquakes
B) Two plant fossils from different continents were similar
C) Continental margins have mountain buildings
D) The frequent eruption of volcanoes around the Pacific Ocean

69

The Earth is made up of different layers, and each layer has its characteristics and boundaries.

Starting from the surface of the Earth, what is the correct order of the Earth's layers?

A) The crust, outer core, inner core, mantle
B) Mantle, outer core, inner core, crust
C) Crust, mantle, outer core, the inner core
D) Outer core, inner core, crust, mantle

70

Which of the following theories explains the formation of the moon?

A) A large object struck Earth, and material from both bodies combined.
B) Gravitational forces attracted materials from outer space.
C) Meteoroids collected and solidified within the pull of Earth's gravity.
D) Gases from Earth escaped from the atmosphere and condensed.

71

What kind of device would an astronomer use in order to determine the composition of a newly discovered star?

A) A device that can determine the direction and velocity of an object.
B) A device that can analyze the frequency of absorbed or emitted light.
C) A device that can calculate the half-life of radioactive elements
D) A device that can magnify an image through a system of multiple lenses.

72

According to the scientists, which of the following is the source of the Earth's magnetic field?

A) The Earth's core has a current of charged particles moving around it
B) The Earth's orbit passes through a stream of charged particles emitted by the sun
C) The Earth's mantle and crust consist of iron-rich magma with charged particles
D) The Earth's core is a large chunk of charged particles

73

Which of the following characteristics of Venus is most directly related to the timing of its appearance at dawn and dusk?

A) Venus is one of the brightest objects in the sky.
B) Venus has a slower rotation time than any other planet in the solar system.
C) The plane of Venus's orbit is tilted relative to the plane of the orbit of Earth.
D) The orbit of Venus is between the sun and the orbit of Earth.

74

Which of the following can be further studied using a handful of information about the cycad fossils found in Arizona during the Triassic Chinle formation?

A) The relationship between the fossils and the pollinators
B) The age of the fossils
C) The location of the North American tectonic plate during that era
D) That region's ancient environment

75

Rocks are always minerals, but not all minerals are rocks.

Which of the following is a not correct explanation about rocks and minerals?

A) A rock can contain minerals whereas a mineral has a unique specific makeup and always has the same composition

B) Both rocks and minerals can contain organic material or fossils of plants and animals.

C) Rocks are always minerals, but not all minerals are rocks. A mineral has a definite chemical composition and a crystalline structure formed by geological processes. Common minerals include quartz, feldspar, mica, amphibole, olivine, and calcite.

D) A rock is an aggregate of one or more minerals whereas a rock may also include organic remains and mineraloids. Common rocks include granite, basalt, limestone, and sandstone.

76

A metamorphic rock is a type of rock which has been changed by extreme heat and pressure. Its name is from 'meta' (meaning change), and 'morph' (meaning form).

Gerold is a meteorologist and he wants to find out if the rock samples collected are metamorphic.

Which of the following is a property of a metamorphic rock?

A) It has tiny holes and spaces.
B) It has interlocking minerals with some foliation.
C) It has straight or wavy stripes of different colors.
D) It has a shiny, smooth surface but without a crystalline structure.

77

The reason why astronomical telescopes designed to receive radio signals often have larger surface areas than optical telescopes is best explained by which of the following statements?

A) Radio waves have greater interference from Earth-based sources than visible light.
B) Visible light has more energy and higher frequency than radio waves.
C) Radio waves do not travel in straight lines while light does.
D) As they pass through Earth's atmosphere, radio waves are refracted less than visible light.

78

The intrusive igneous rocks that are composed of unusually large crystals are called pegmatites.

Which condition can typically result in the formation of pegmatites?

A) The solidification of magma bodies below the extinct volcanoes
B) The crystallization of rocks at slow rates and the high temperatures near the boundary between the mantle and the crust
C) The solidification of the granitic batholiths, leaving fluid-rich residual melt
D) The crystallization at relatively fast rates as magma flows rapidly away from its source to form a sill

CONTINUE ▶

79

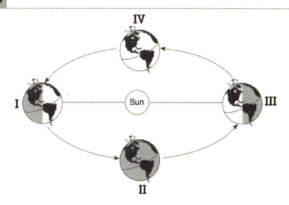

The figure above shows Earth orbiting the Sun while it is rotating about its axis once every 24 hours.

Which change in seasons occurs in the Northern Hemisphere at position IV?

A) Winter is ending, and spring is beginning.
B) Spring is ending, and summer is beginning.
C) Summer is ending, and fall is beginning.
D) Fall is ending, and winter is beginning.

80

In which of the following areas of Earth and space research is the analysis of the ratio of the oxygen isotopes O-18 and O-16 extremely useful?

A) Calculating the age of lava flows from Pleistocene era volcanic eruptions
B) Determining relative changes in global temperature during the Quaternary period
C) Calculating the concentration of carbon dioxide in gas bubbles trapped in ice sheets
D) Determining sedimentation rates on the abyssal plains of the deep oceans

81

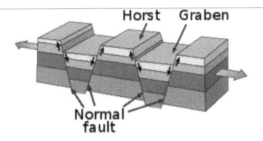

In geology, horst and graben refer to regions that lie between normal faults and are either higher or lower than the area beyond the faults.

The formation of the horst and graben structures of the Basin and Range Province of the western United States was a result of which of the following?

A) The differential erosion of sedimentary rocks and volcanic rocks for the past million years
B) The tensional forces that caused the occurrence of crustal extension of the North American Plate
C) The erosion and deposition cycles associated with the multiple glaciations during the Pleistocene period
D) The compressional forces that caused the uplift of the North American Plate

82

According to an Arabic scholar Avicenna, mountains could only be formed over long periods of time. He supported his hypothesis with his firsthand knowledge based on several observations of geologic processes such as water erosion and the localized uplift caused by earthquakes.

Which geologic principle fundamental to modern geology did Avicenna employ to understand geologic past?

A) The original horizontality principle
B) The superposition principle
C) The cross-cutting relationships principle
D) The uniformitarianism principle

Many of the mountaintops in the Sierra Nevada mountain range are exposed granitic batholiths that have eroded into rounded domes, known as exfoliation domes.

What process could have led to the formation of these exfoliation domes?

A) The sheeting of substantial concentric slabs due to the unloading of pressure
B) The chemical weathering of potassium ions found in the surface of rocks
C) The erosion of granite during high runoff periods
D) The fluctuation of temperatures causing the rock face to shrink and swell

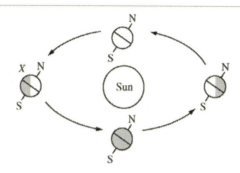

Earth's orbit around the Sun is given above. Which of the following is true of the Earth at location X?

A) The spring equinox occurs.
B) The fall equinox occurs.
C) The winter solstice occurs in the northern hemisphere.
D) The summer solstice occurs in the northern hemisphere.

85

Which of the following elements is present in the largest amount of rocks and minerals?

A) Carbon
B) Silicon
C) Hydrogen
D) Aluminum

86

Among the following events, which one would be least likely to occur at a significantly smaller scale?

A) Sediment is formed into a stream due to the erosion of a hillside.
B) A star is formed from an interstellar dust cloud due to gravitational attraction.
C) The discharge of static electricity produces a lightning bolt during a storm.
D) The electric currents in the Earth's outer core generate a magnetic field.

SECTION 3 - EARTH & SPACE SCIENCE

#	Answer	Topic	Subtopic	#	Answer	Topic	Subtopic	#	Answer	Topic	Subtopic	#	Answer	Topic	Subtopic
1	A	TB	S1	23	D	TB	S1	45	C	TB	S1	67	A	TB	S1
2	D	TB	S1	24	B	TB	S1	46	D	TB	S1	68	B	TB	S1
3	A	TB	S1	25	A	TB	S1	47	D	TB	S1	69	C	TB	S1
4	B	TB	S1	26	B	TB	S1	48	D	TB	S1	70	A	TB	S2
5	C	TB	S1	27	A	TB	S1	49	B	TB	S1	71	B	TB	S2
6	A	TB	S1	28	D	TB	S1	50	A	TB	S1	72	A	TB	S1
7	D	TB	S1	29	B	TB	S1	51	C	TB	S1	73	D	TB	S2
8	A	TB	S1	30	D	TB	S1	52	B	TB	S1	74	D	TB	S1
9	A	TB	S1	31	D	TB	S1	53	C	TB	S1	75	B	TB	S1
10	D	TB	S1	32	D	TB	S1	54	C	TB	S2	76	B	TB	S1
11	B	TB	S1	33	D	TB	S1	55	D	TB	S1	77	B	TB	S2
12	D	TB	S1	34	C	TB	S1	56	A	TB	S1	78	C	TB	S1
13	B	TB	S1	35	D	TB	S1	57	D	TB	S2	79	D	TB	S2
14	C	TB	S2	36	A	TB	S2	58	A	TB	S2	80	B	TB	S1
15	A	TB	S1	37	B	TB	S1	59	C	TB	S1	81	B	TB	S1
16	C	TB	S1	38	A	TB	S1	60	D	TB	S1	82	D	TB	S1
17	A	TB	S1	39	C	TB	S2	61	A	TB	S1	83	A	TB	S1
18	D	TB	S1	40	A	TB	S1	62	C	TB	S1	84	A	TB	S2
19	A	TB	S1	41	C	TB	S1	63	C	TB	S1	85	A	TB	S1
20	C	TB	S1	42	A	TB	S1	64	B	TB	S1	86	B	TB	S1
21	B	TB	S1	43	C	TB	S1	65	A	TB	S1				
22	D	TB	S1	44	D	TB	S1	66	A	TB	S2				

Topics & Subtopics

Code	Description
SB1	Geology & Atmosphere
SB2	Astronomy

Code	Description
TB	Earth & Space Science

TEST DIRECTION

DIRECTIONS

Read the questions carefully and then choose the ONE best answer to each question.

Be sure to allocate your time carefully so you are able to complete the entire test within the testing session. You may go back and review your answers at any time.

You may use any available space in your test booklet for scratch work.

Questions in this booklet are not actual test questions but they are the samples for commonly asked questions.

This test aims to cover all topics which may appear on the actual test. However some topics may not be covered.

Studying this booklet will be preparing you for the actual test. It will not guarantee improving your test score but it will help you pass your exam on the first attempt.

Some useful tips for answering multiple choice questions;

- Start with the questions that you can easily answer.

- Underline the keywords in the question.

- Be sure to read all the choices given.

- Watch for keywords such as NOT, always, only, all, never, completely.

- Do not forget to answer every question.

1

$$Al_2O_3$$

The atomic mass of aluminum is 27 g/mol and the atomic mass of oxygen is 16 g/mol. What is the molar mass of aluminum oxide whose formula is given above?

A) 102 g
B) 113 g
C) 135 g
D) 215 g

2

When a balloon, which is full of air, is heated from room temperature to 60 Celcius degree, its volume increases.

Which of the following gas laws explains this phenomenon?

A) Boyle's Law
B) Charles Law
C) Kelvin's Law
D) Gay Lussac's Law

3

$$3CO_2 + 2H_2O \rightarrow C_3H_4 + 5O_2$$

$$2H_2 + 2O_2 \rightarrow 2H_2O$$

$$3H_2 + 2N_2 \rightarrow 2NH_3$$

$$H_2 + Cl_2 \rightarrow 2HCl$$

How many of the chemical equations given above (is) are balanced?

A) 1
B) 2
C) 3
D) 4

4

At room temperature a basic solution can have which of the following pH values?

A) 3.0
B) 5.0
C) 7.0
D) 9.0

5

STP in chemistry is the abbreviation for Standard Temperature and Pressure. It is most commonly used when performing calculations on gases.

Which of the following defines STP?

A) 0 K and 1.0 atm pressure.
B) 0 °C and 1.0 atm pressure.
C) 0 °C and 273 mm Hg pressure.
D) 0 K and 760 cm Hg pressure.

6

Ionization energy in kJ/mol	1st	2nd	3rd	4th
	578	1817	2745	11580

Ionization energies of an element is given above. How many valence electrons does this element have?

A) 1
B) 2
C) 3
D) 4

7

Which of the following about covalent bonds is not correct?

A) Electrons are shared to hold the atoms together in a bond.
B) They have lower melting and boiling points than ionic compounds.
C) They do not break apart into ions when dissolved in water.
D) They tend to be solid at room temperature.

8

Carbon atoms have 6 protons and 6 neutrons and 6 electrons. Hydrogen atoms have 1 proton and 1 electron. One carbon atom is about how many times more massive than one hydrogen atom?

A) 3
B) 4
C) 6
D) 12

CONTINUE ▶

9

A chemical change is a chemical reaction in which the original properties of matter are changed and at least one new substance is formed. The formation of rust on iron is a chemical change.

Which of the following statements about chemical change is true?

A) A chemical change is easily reversible.
B) A chemical change only involves changing states of matter.
C) A chemical change happens faster than a physical change.
D) A chemical change involves breaking and forming of chemical bonds.

10

$$Avagadro's\ Number(N) = 6.02 \cdot 10^{23}$$

In 1909, French physicist Jean Perrin proposed Avogadro's number. He won the 1926 Nobel Prize in physics. In chemistry and physics, Avogadro's number usually refers to the quantity of atoms, molecules, or ions.

Carbon atom has 6 protons, 6 neutrons, and 6 electrons. 36g Carbon contains how many Carbon atom?

A) 1 N
B) 3 N
C) 4 N
D) 6 N

11

Some chemistry terms are defined below. Which of the following is not a correct definition?

A) The attraction of an atom for shared electrons is called electronegativity.
B) The attraction of an atom for an additional electron is called electron attraction.
C) The distance from the nucleus to the outermost electron is known as the atomic radius.
D) Valence electrons are those electrons that reside in the outermost shell surrounding an atomic nucleus.

12

$$xCO_2 + yH_2O \rightarrow C_6H_{12}O_6 + zO_2$$

Photosynthesis is a reaction which allows plants to use sunlight to produce food and oxygen.

Chemical equation of photosynthesis is given above. After you balance the equation, what is the sum of $x + y + z$?

A) 6
B) 12
C) 15
D) 18

13

A double replacement reaction involves "replacing" two elements in the reactants, with two in the products.

A single replacement reaction involves the "replacing" of an element in the reactants with another element in the products.

There are different types of chemical reactions. Two of them are defined above. Which of the following about the types of chemical reactions is not correct?

A) When two simple substances combine to produce a single more complex substance, this reaction is called synthesis.
B) If one species is oxidized in a reaction, another must be reduced. These type of reactions are called replacement reactions.
C) A decomposition reaction is the reverse of a synthesis (combination) reaction. It is the breakdown of a chemical compound into individual elements.
D) Combustion reactions almost always involve oxygen, and are almost always exothermic, meaning they produce heat. Chemical reactions that give off light and heat are referred to as "burning."

14

The atomic theory, which holds that matter is composed of tiny, indivisible particles was first proposed by the Greek philosopher Democritus.

Which of the following about the modern atomic theories of the atom is not correct?

A) Solid sphere model, which is proposed by John Dalton in 1808, states that an atom is a solid sphere that could not be divided into smaller particles.
B) The plum pudding model, which is proposed by J. J. Thomson in 1904, states that electrons are negatively-charged particles and atoms are neutrally-charged.
C) Nuclear model, which is proposed by Ernest Rutherford in 1911, states that nearly all of the mass of the atom is located in a nucleus at the center of the atom.
D) Bohr model, which is proposed by Neils Bohr in 1913, states that the negatively-charged electrons orbit in the electron clouds (orbitals).

15

Which of the following quantities is everytime conserved in chemical reactions?

A) Mass
B) Volume
C) Formula units
D) Number of moles

16

Phase changes occur when sufficient energy is supplied to the system or removed from the system. It also occurs when the pressure on the system is changed.

In which of the following phase change, energy is released?

A) When snow melts after hitting the ground.
B) When water evaporates from the surface of the lake.
C) When water boils and turns into steam.
D) When dew forms on grass in the morning.

17

Which of the following reactions does not produce hydrogen gas?

A) Electrolysis of water
B) Decomposition of ammonia
C) The reaction of hydrochloric acid with zinc
D) The reaction of sulphuric acid with sodium hydroxide

18

$$HCl + NaOH \rightarrow NaCl + H_2O$$

$$2H_2 + O_2 \rightarrow 2H_2O$$

$$3H_2 + 2N_2 \rightarrow 2NH_3$$

$$H_2 + Cl_2 \rightarrow 2HCl$$

Different types of reactions are given above. What type of reaction is not given above?

A) Acid - Base reaction
B) Combustion
C) Synthesis
D) Decomposition

$$^{23}_{11}X \rightarrow {}^{23}_{10}Y + ?$$

A radioactive decay reaction is given above. Which of the following is the missing product in the nuclear reaction?

A) Positron
B) Beta particle
C) Gamma ray
D) Alpha particle

20

- Chromatography is a laboratory technique to separate mixtures. It is defined as the separation of the components of a mixture by slow passage over or through a material that absorbs the components differently.

- A characteristic feature of any form of chromatography is the use of a mobile and a stationary phase.

- It was first employed by the Italian-born scientist Mikhail Tsvet in 1900. Tsvet continued to work with chromatography in the first decade of the 20th century, primarily for the separation of plant pigments such as chlorophyll, carotenes, and xanthophylls.

Chromatography is briefly explained above. Which of the following explanations about chromatography is not correct?

A) The solution in paper chromatography moves up the paper by capillary action.

B) All forms of chromatography use a stationary phase to carry the mixture over or through a mobile phase. In the stationary phase, the mixture is dissolved in the fluid.

C) In chromatography, solution seeps through an adsorbent (such as clay, gel, or paper) so each compound becomes adsorbed into a separate, often colored, layer.

D) The factors effective on the chromatography process include molecular characteristics related to adsorption (liquid-solid), partition (liquid-solid), and affinity or differences among their molecular weights.

21

By the expansion process, gases take the shape of their container. Which of the following about the gases is not correct?

A) Effusion refers to the movement of gas particles through a small hole. Air slowly escaping from a pinhole in a tire is an example for effusion.

B) Diffusion occurs when gas molecules disperse throughout a container. The odor of perfume spreading throughout a room is an example of diffusion.

C) Graham's Law states that the effusion rate of a gas is directly proportional to the square root of the mass of its particles.

D) Diffusion is faster at higher temperatures because the gas molecules have greater kinetic energy.

22

Which of the following statement regarding the first ionization energy of metals and nonmetals in the same period is correct?

A) Nonmetals usually have higher ionization energies because they usually have bigger atomic radius.
B) Nonmetals usually have higher ionization energies because they are closer to having filled a complete energy level.
C) Metals usually have higher ionization energies because they usually have smaller atomic radius.
D) Metals usually have higher ionization energies because they usually have more protons than nonmetals.

23

Molarity is used to express the concentration of a solution. It is the number of moles of solute (the material dissolved) per liter of solution.

What is the molarity of 5.00 g of NaOH in 750.0 ml of solution?

(Na=23g/mole, H=1 g/mole, O=16g/mole)

A) 0.125 M
B) 0.166 M
C) 6.666 M
D) 10.66 M

24

Hydrogen bonding results from the attractive force between a hydrogen atom that is covalently bonded to a very electronegative atom such as an N, O, or F.

Hydrogen bonding is a special case of which of the following?

A) Ionic bonding
B) Ion-ion interactions
C) Dipole-dipole attractions
D) London-dispersion forces

25

Some reactions take hundreds, maybe even thousands, of years while others can happen in less than one second. If a reaction has a high rate, that means the molecules combine at a higher speed than a reaction with a slow rate.

Which of the following does not define the reaction rate?

A) It is the speed at which reactants are converted into products.

B) It is the measure of the chemical change of the reactants.

C) It is the measure of the change in concentration of the reactants per unit time.

D) It is the measure of the change in concentration of the products per unit time.

26

Which of the following has the largest first ionization energy?

A) Na
B) Mg
C) Al
D) Ar

27

Elleny determines that 1.26 g of iron reacts with 0.54 g of oxygen to form rust. What is the percent composition of oxygen in the new compound?

A) 23.3%
B) 30%
C) 42.8%
D) 70%

28

Which of the following is true when materials combine to form a mixture?

A) They combine in a specific ratio.
B) They keep their original properties.
C) They always change their physical state.
D) They react to form a new substance with new properties.

CONTINUE ▶

29

When a basic solution is titrated with drops of acid, how does the pH value of the solution change?

A) It increases.
B) It decreases.
C) It stays same.
D) It approaches to 14.

30

Which of the following solutions will have the highest boiling point at room temperature?

A) 20 g water containing 6 g salt
B) 50 g water containing 13 g salt
C) 100 g water containing 25 g salt
D) 200 g water containing 45g salt

31

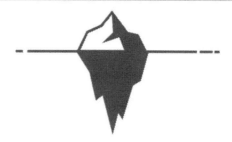

In general, intramolecular forces determine the chemical properties of a substance and intermolecular forces determine its physical properties.

Which of the following intermolecular forces is responsible for the fact that ice is less dense than liquid water?

A) Ionic bonding
B) Hydrogen bonding
C) Dipole-dipole forces
D) London dispersion forces

32

According to the kinetic-molecular theory, which of the following is not correct?

A) Gas particles move in predictable patterns.
B) Gas particles move independently of each other.
C) Gas particles are spaced far apart from each other.
D) Particles of solids, liquids, and gases are in constant motion.

33

Which of the following explains how atomic masses vary throughout the periodic table of the elements?

A) Atomic masses increase from top to bottom and left to right.
B) Atomic masses increase from bottom to top and left to right.
C) Atomic masses increase from top to bottom and right to left.
D) Atomic masses increase from bottom to top and right to left.

34

$$C_3H_8 + O_2 \rightarrow CO_2 + H_2O$$

The chemical equation given above represents the combustion of propane. When correctly balanced, what is the coefficient of oxygen?

A) 3
B) 4
C) 5
D) 10

35

$$^{200}_{80}X^{+2}$$

Which of the following gives the correct number of proton, neutron, and electron of the ion given above?

A) 80 proton, 200 neutron, 82 electron
B) 80 proton, 200 neutron, 78 electron
C) 80 proton, 120 neutron, 78 electron
D) 80 proton, 120 neutron, 82 electron

36

Which of the following is an example of exothermic physical process?

A) Melting of ice
B) Combustion of gasoline
C) Photosynthesis of glucose
D) Condensation of water vapor

37

$$^{210}_{84}\text{Pb} \rightarrow \,^{M}_{N}\text{Pb} + \,^{4}_{2}\text{He}$$

Alpha decay occurs when a nucleus is unstable because it has too many protons. During α-decay, an atomic nucleus emits an alpha particle. An α-particle is a helium nucleus which contains 2 protons and 2 neutrons, for a mass number of 4.

If Polonium-214 undergoes alpha decay, what will be the values of M and N?

A) M = 210, N = 84
B) M = 214, N = 86
C) M = 206, N = 82
D) M = 206, N = 86

38

An atom has seven electrons in a 3d subshell. How many orbitals in this subshell have an unpaired electron?

A) 1
B) 2
C) 3
D) 4

39

Which of the following about ionic bonds is not correct?

A) Ionic bonds have high melting points.
B) Metals lose electrons, nonmetals gain electron.
C) Ions with opposite charges hold ionic bonds together.
D) An ionic bond is a sharing of electrons.

40

Which of the following about ionization energy is not correct?

A) Low ionization energy is a general characteristic of metals.
B) Ionization energy is the energy required to remove an electron from an atom.
C) Ionization energies generally tend to increase across a period of the periodic table from right to left.
D) The energy needed to remove the most loosely held electron from a neutral atom is called first ionization energy.

41

Both fission and fusion are nuclear processes by which atoms are altered to create energy.

Which of the following statements best describes the difference between nuclear fission and nuclear fusion reactions?

A) Fission generates heat energy, and fusion generates kinetic energy.
B) Fission forms heavier elements and fusion forms lighter elements.
C) Nuclei gain electrons during fission and release electrons during fusion.
D) Fission is the division of one atom into two, and fusion is the combination of two lighter atoms into a larger one.

42

Gay-Lussac's law was found by Joseph Louis Gay-Lussac in 1808.

Which of the following is true according to Gay-Lussac's Law?

A) The volume of a gas in a closed container is directly proportional to its absolute temperature.
B) The volume of a gas in a closed container is directly proportional to its absolute pressure.
C) The pressure of a given amount of gas held at constant volume is directly proportional to the Kelvin temperature.
D) The pressure exerted by the gas on the sides of its container is inversely proportional to its absolute temperature.

43

Vapor pressure and volatility are liquid properties related to evaporation. Which of the following explanation about these concepts is not correct?

A) Volatility and vapor pressure are inversely proportional to one another.
B) Water can boil at 105°C if the air pressure on the water is increased.
C) When the vapor pressure of a liquid is less than the atmospheric pressure, the liquid boils.
D) Cooking at high altitudes take longer than at low altitudes because water boils at a lower temperature at high altitude than at low altitude.

44

In chemistry, colligative properties are the properties of solutions that depend on the ratio of the number of solute particles to the number of solvent molecules in a solution.

Dissolving table salt in water elevates the boiling point of the salt solution. Boiling point is most directly affected by which of the following factors?

A) The reactivity of sodium and chloride ions
B) The specific heat capacity of the solution
C) The concentration of the solute dissolved in the solution
D) The reduced hydrogen bonding between water molecules

45

Empirical Formula : C_2H_3
Molecular Formula : C_xH_y

An organic compound's molecular and emprical formulas are given above. If the compound has a molecular mass of 81 g/mole, what is the sum of $x + y$?

(C = 12g/mole, H = 1 g/mole)

A) 5
B) 10
C) 15
D) 20

46

Which of the following is the ratio of the actual yield to the theoretical yield?

A) Real yield
B) Percent yield
C) Experimental yield
D) Stoichiometric yield

47

When Ernest Rutherford shot a beam of alpha particles at a sheet of gold foil, a few of the particles were deflected. He established the nuclear theory of the atom with his **gold-foil experiment**.

Which of the following is a conclusion of gold foil experiment?

A) Atom is mostly empty space with a dense, positively charged nucleus.
B) Atom is a hard, indivisible sphere which contains protons, neutrons, and electrons.
C) A negatively charged nucleus is surrounded by mostly empty space.
D) An electron has properties of both waves and particles.

48

Which of the following explains Boyle's Law?

A) The pressure of a given mass of an ideal gas is inversely proportional to its volume at a constant temperature.
B) The volume of an ideal gas at constant pressure is directly proportional to the absolute temperature.
C) The pressure exerted by the gas on the sides of its container is directly proportional to its absolute temperature.
D) Equal volumes of gases at the same temperature and pressure contain equal numbers of molecules.

49

The term "ion" was introduced by English chemist and physicist Michael Faraday in 1834 to describe the chemical particles that travel from one electrode to another in the aqueous solution. The word ion comes from the Greek word ienai, which means "to go".

Which of the following about the ions is not correct?

A) Negative ions are called anions, positive ions are called cations.
B) An ion is an atom (or group of atoms) that has a positive or negative charge.
C) A positive ion and a negative ion come together to form covalent bonding.
D) Positive and negative ions are formed when electrons are transferred (lost or gained) between atoms.

50

$C_3H_8 + 5O_2 \rightarrow 3CO_2 + 4H_2O$

$H_2O \rightarrow 2H_2 + O_2$

$C_6H_{12}O_6 + 6O_2 \rightarrow 6CO_2 + 6H_2O$

$2NH_3 \rightarrow 3H_2 + N_2$

How many of the chemical reactions given above is (are) a combustion reaction?

A) 1
B) 2
C) 3
D) 4

51

Which combination below corresponds to a cation with a +1 charge?

A) 11 proton, 11 electron, 12 neutron
B) 13 proton, 11 electron, 12 neutron
C) 16 proton, 18 electron, 15 neutron
D) 14 proton, 13 electron, 16 neutron

52

Which of the following best explains the high melting point of diamond?

A) Three-dimensional crystal structure.
B) Strong covalent bonds between carbon atoms.
C) Strong Van der Waals bonds between carbon atoms.
D) Strong ionic bonds between carbon atoms.

53

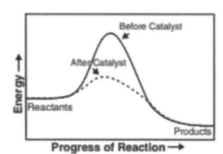

A **catalyst** is a substance that increases the rate of a chemical reaction without itself undergoing any permanent chemical change.

How can a catalyst speed up the rate of a chemical reaction?

A) By increasing the equilibrium constant in favor of products.
B) By raising the temperature at which the reaction occurs.
C) By increasing the pressure of reactants, thus favoring products.
D) By lowering the activation energy that is required for the reaction to occur.

54

- Heat of Fusion of water: 80 cal/g
- Heat of Vaporization of water: 540 cal/g
- Specific Heat of water: 1cal/g °C

How much heat must be added to 10 grams of ice at 0°C to convert it to water vapor at 100°C?

A) 800 cal
B) 1,800 cal
C) 6,400 cal
D) 7,200 cal

55

$^{85}Rb \to 72.2\%$ $^{87}Rb \to 27.8\%$

Rubidium has two common isotopes. What is the average atomic mass of rubidium according to the relative abundances of the isotopes given above?

A) 85.55
B) 86.44
C) 85.12
D) 86.42

56

The strength of the intermolecular forces between solutes and solvents determines the solubility of a given solute in a given solvent. In general, **"Like dissolves like"** is a rule used by chemists to explain how some solvents work.

Which of the following fact does the phrase "like dissolves like" refer to?

A) Liquids can only dissolve other liquids.
B) Solvents can only dissolve solutes of similar molecular weight.
C) Polar solvents dissolve polar solutes, and nonpolar solvents dissolve nonpolar solutes.
D) Polar solvents can only dissolve nonpolar solutes and nonpolar solvents can only dissolve polar solutes.

57

A solution is defined as a homogeneous mixture of two or more substances in which the minor component (the solute) is uniformly distributed within the major component (the solvent).

Which of the following statements about the solutions is not correct?

A) Solubility is the ability for a given substance, the solute, to dissolve in a solvent.
B) When vitamin B is dissolved in water, water is the the solvent and vitamin B is the solute.
C) Concentration refers to the amount of a substance per defined space. It is usually expressed in terms of mass per unit volume.
D) If the solubility of N is 20g per 100g of water at a certain temperature, then the percentage of N in a saturated solution is 20%

58

M is an acid with a pH of 2 and N is another acid with a pH of 5.

Which of the following about the strengths of these acids is correct?

A) M is a thousand times stronger than N.
B) N is a thousand times stronger than M.
C) M is three times stronger than N.
D) N is three times stronger than M.

59

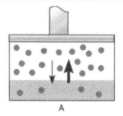 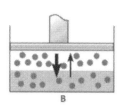

According to the diagrams of gas-liquid solution given above, which of the following about the solubility of the gas in the liquid is correct?

A) Solubility of gas increases as the pressure of the gas above the liquid increases.
B) Solubility of gas increases as the pressure of the gas above the liquid decreases.
C) Solubility of gas decreases as the pressure of the gas above the liquid increases.
D) Solubility of gas decreases as the pressure of the gas above the liquid decreases.

60

Which of the following bonds is most ionic?

A) Na - Cl
B) H - Cl
C) F - Cl
D) K - Cl

61

Which of the following explains the primary significance of Rutherford's Gold Foil experiment?

A) It proves the concept of radioactive decay.
B) It measured the electric charge of a single electron.
C) It created new radioactive isotopes by nuclear reactions.
D) It proves the existence of a small, dense, positively charged atomic nucleus.

62

A compound contains 1.2 moles of carbon and 3.2 moles of hydrogen. What is the percent composition by mass of carbon in the compound? (C = 12g/mole, H = 1 g/mole)

A) 27.3%
B) 37.5%
C) 81.8%
D) 92.3%

63

Which of the following about the basic terms of solutions is not correct?

A) Mass Percent = mass of solution / mass of solute
B) Molality = Moles of solute / Kg of Solvent (abbreviation = m)
C) Molarity = Moles of solute / Liters of Solution (abbreviation = M)
D) Normality = Equivalents of solute / Molarity of Solution (abbreviation = N)

64

Which of the following properties generally decreases when moving left to right across a period of the periodic table?

A) Atomic radius
B) Electron affinity
C) Ionization energy
D) Number of valence electrons

65

Which of the following explains why the table of elements is called "the periodic table"?

A) Because the rows are called periods.
B) Because it describes the periodic recurrence of physical properties of the elements.
C) Because it describes the periodic recurrence of chemical properties of the elements.
D) Because the elements are grouped as metals, metalloids, and non-metals.

66

If a gas with a pressure of 2.0 atm expands into a volume that is twice its original volume, and the gas is heated from 100.0 K to 300.0 K, what is the final pressure of the gas?

A) 1.0 atm
B) 3.0 atm
C) 6.0 atm
D) 12.0 atm

CONTINUE ▶

67

Which of the following is not an observable property of many bases?

A) When mixed with acids they can produce salts.
B) When they react with water they become slippery.
C) When they are mixed with water they release hydrogen ion.
D) When they are mixed with water their pH decreases.

68

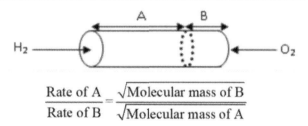

$$\frac{\text{Rate of A}}{\text{Rate of B}} = \frac{\sqrt{\text{Molecular mass of B}}}{\sqrt{\text{Molecular mass of A}}}$$

The speed of the molecules in a gas is inversely proportional to the square root of the mass of its particles.

Both gases, hydrogen and oxygen, are spread at the same time through the glass tube with the length of 25 cm as it is shown above. If gases are at the same temperature and meet at the dotted region, what is the length of A? (The molar mass of hydrogen gas is 2g per mole, and the molar mass of oxygen is 32g per mole)

A) 5 cm
B) 6.25 cm
C) 18.75 cm
D) 20 cm

69

Electronegativity is a measure of the tendency of an atom to attract a bonding pair of electrons.

Which of the following elements is the most electronegative?

A) Hydrogen
B) Florine
C) Francium
D) Caesium

70

Which of the following about Sodium and Chlorine is true?

A) Sodium has a larger first ionization energy and a greater electronegativity.
B) Sodium has a bigger atomic radius and a greater electron affinity.
C) Chlorine has a bigger electronegativity and larger first ionization energy.
D) Chlorine has a bigger atomic radius and smaller first ionization energy.

71

$$\frac{\text{Rate of A}}{\text{Rate of B}} = \frac{\sqrt{\text{Molecular mass of B}}}{\sqrt{\text{Molecular mass of A}}}$$

Gases move from high to low concentrations. According to Graham's Law of Effusion, at the same conditions of temperature, lighter gases effuse faster.

A molecule of oxygen gas has an average speed of 10 m/s at a given temperature and pressure. What is the average speed of hydrogen molecules at the same conditions? (O = 16g/mole, H = 1 g/mole)

A) 5 m/s
B) 20 m/s
C) 40 m/s
D) 80 m/s

72

Which of the following has the biggest atomic radius?

A) Li
B) K
C) Rb
D) Cs

73

The roots of the word "isomer" are Greek; "isos + meros", or "equal parts." Isomerism was first noticed in 1827, by German Chemist Friedrich Woehler when he prepared silver cyanate.

Which of the following defines isomers?

A) They are the molecules with the same molecular formula but a different overall charge.
B) They are the molecules with the same net dipole but different atoms involved in the bond.
C) They are the compounds with the same formula but a different arrangement of atoms.
D) They are the molecules with the same number of electrons and protons but a different number of neutrons.

74

$$2H_2O \rightarrow 2H_2 + O_2$$

Electrolysis refers to the use of electricity to drive a chemical reaction that would not normally occur on its own.

Electrolysis of water is the decomposition of water into oxygen and hydrogen gas due to the passage of an electric current.

In the electrolysis of water, how many grams of oxygen gas will be produced if 6 grams of hydrogen gas is formed according to the equation given above?
(O = 16 g/mole, H = 1 g/mole)

A) 24 g
B) 32 g
C) 48 g
D) 72 g

75

$$2Al + 6HCl \rightarrow 2AlCl_3 + 3H_2$$

When strips of aluminum are placed in hydrochloric acid, aluminum chloride and hydrogen gas are produced. According to the balanced equation given above, what type of reaction is this?

A) Acid-base
B) Single-replacement
C) Double-replacement
D) Combustion

76

$$PV = nRT$$

What is the volume of a 3 mole sample of a gas at 35°C and 2.0 atm according to the ideal gas law given above? (R = 22.4/273)

A) 0.52 L
B) 4 L
C) 37.9 L
D) 77.8 L

SECTION 4 - CHEMISTRY

#	Answer	Topic	Subtopic	#	Answer	Topic	Subtopic	#	Answer	Topic	Subtopic	#	Answer	Topic	Subtopic
1	A	TB	S4	20	B	TB	S3	39	D	TB	S1	58	A	TB	S2
2	B	TB	S8	21	C	TB	S8	40	C	TB	S7	59	A	TB	S3
3	A	TB	S5	22	B	TB	S7	41	D	TB	S10	60	D	TB	S1
4	D	TB	S2	23	B	TB	S3	42	C	TB	S8	61	D	TB	S7
5	B	TB	S8	24	C	TB	S8	43	A	TB	S3	62	C	TB	S1
6	C	TB	S7	25	B	TB	S5	44	C	TB	S3	63	A	TB	S3
7	D	TB	S1	26	D	TB	S7	45	C	TB	S1	64	A	TB	S7
8	D	TB	S7	27	B	TB	S1	46	B	TB	S4	65	C	TB	S7
9	D	TB	S6	28	B	TB	S3	47	A	TB	S7	66	B	TB	S8
10	B	TB	S4	29	B	TB	S2	48	A	TB	S8	67	C	TB	S2
11	B	TB	S7	30	A	TB	S3	49	C	TB	S7	68	D	TB	S8
12	D	TB	S5	31	B	TB	S8	50	B	TB	S5	69	B	TB	S7
13	B	TB	S5	32	A	TB	S8	51	D	TB	S7	70	C	TB	S7
14	D	TB	S7	33	A	TB	S7	52	B	TB	S7	71	C	TB	S8
15	A	TB	S5	34	C	TB	S5	53	D	TB	S5	72	D	TB	S7
16	D	TB	S8	35	C	TB	S7	54	D	TB	S8	73	C	TB	S6
17	D	TB	S5	36	D	TB	S6	55	A	TB	S7	74	C	TB	S10
18	D	TB	S5	37	C	TB	S10	56	C	TB	S3	75	B	TB	S5
19	A	TB	S10	38	C	TB	S7	57	D	TB	S3	76	C	TB	S8

Topics & Subtopics

Code	Description	Code	Description
SB1	Compounds	SB5	Chemical Reactions
SB10	Electrochemistry and Nuclear Chemistry	SB6	Introduction to Chemistry
SB2	Acids and Bases	SB7	Atoms, Elements, and Periodic Table
SB3	Mixtures and Solutions	SB8	States of Matter and Intermolecular Forces
SB4	Mole Concept and Stoichiometry	TB	CHEMISTRY

TEST DIRECTION

DIRECTIONS

Read the questions carefully and then choose the ONE best answer to each question.

Be sure to allocate your time carefully so you are able to complete the entire test within the testing session. You may go back and review your answers at any time.

You may use any available space in your test booklet for scratch work.

Questions in this booklet are not actual test questions but they are the samples for commonly asked questions.

This test aims to cover all topics which may appear on the actual test. However some topics may not be covered.

Studying this booklet will be preparing you for the actual test. It will not guarantee improving your test score but it will help you pass your exam on the first attempt.

Some useful tips for answering multiple choice questions;

- Start with the questions that you can easily answer.

- Underline the keywords in the question.

- Be sure to read all the choices given.

- Watch for keywords such as NOT, always, only, all, never, completely.

- Do not forget to answer every question.

1

Which of the following ecological activities would most likely result in an increase in the amount of phosphorous available to organisms in an ecosystem?

A) Cultivation of leguminous plants
B) Rising of air temperature
C) Weathering of rocks
D) The burning of fossil fuels

2

Grass → Insect → Frog → Snake → Eagle

Food chain, in ecology, is a linear network of links in a food web showing the sequence of transfer of matter and energy in the form of food from organism to organism.

Which of the following can be a correct sequence in the food chain which is given above?

A) mice > green plants > snake > hawk
B) green plants > mice > snake > hawk
C) green plants > snake > mice > hawk
D) hawk > snake > mice > green plants

3

1. High humidity and temperature stability are present.

2. Hot, moist biome found near Earth's equator.

3. The world's largest ones are in South America, Africa, and Southeast Asia.

4. Receive from 60 to 160 inches of precipitation that is fairly evenly distributed throughout the year.

Which of the following is defined above?

A) Taiga (Boreal forests)
B) Deciduous forest
C) Temperate forests
D) Tropical rainforest

4

A **predator** is an organism that eats another organism. The **prey** is the organism which the **predator** eats.

In an ecosystem, which of the following would most likely occur?

A) When the number of prey increases, then the number of predator decreases.
B) When the number of prey increases, then the number of predator increases.
C) When the number of prey decreases, then the number of predator increases.
D) When the number of predator decreases, then the number of prey decreases.

5

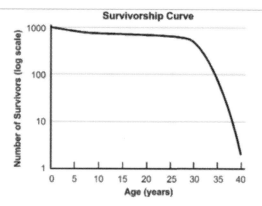

Which of the following best explains the survivorship curve given regarding a population made up of individuals with an average life expectancy of 40 years?

A) During middle age, the population has a low mortality rate.
B) Individuals start reproduction very early in the lifespan.
C) During infancy, members of the population are most vulnerable.
D) At the end of the lifespan, there is a great increase in survivorship.

The genotype is the part of the genetic makeup of a cell which determines the phenotype.

Which of the following options reveals the fact that natural selection affects the phenotype of an individual rather than its genotype?

A) Harmful recessive alleles are removed from a population in a more difficult way than harmful dominant alleles.
B) Varieties in the behavior of individuals in a population are highly affected by the dissimilarities in genotypes in the population.
C) Individuals who are genetically similar may differ in their phenotypes if they grow and develop under unalike environmental conditions.
D) A characteristic that is selectively neutral may increase in frequency in a population if it is genetically related to a second characteristic which increases the fitness of the individual.

Lamarck believed that if an organism changes during life to adapt to its environment, those changes are passed on to its offspring.

According to Lamark, evolution occured as a result of which of the following?

A) Recapitulation
B) Overproduction
C) Blending inheritance
D) Inheritance of acquired characteristics

Phytoplankton are microscopic organisms that reside near the ocean's surface, where they soak up the sunshine.

Which of the following about phytoplankton is not correct?

A) Phytoplankton help in balancing the Earth's climate.

B) Phytoplankton contain chloroplast and require sunlight to do photosynthesis.

C) Phytoplankton are microscopic marine algae which are the base of several aquatic food webs.

D) Phytoplankton are the most important primary producers in the ocean, base of the oceanic food chain, and important component of the global carbon cycle.

Sometimes, organisms have to share the same resources and they avoid competition by isolating themselves from each other.

Which of the following about the isolation is not correct?

A) Geographic Isolation occurs when livings are not in the same place at the same time.

B) By day, birds rule the air. By night, however, bats rule the roost. This is an example of geographic isolation.

C) Mechanical Isolation occurs when morphological differences directly livings to avoid competition with others.

D) Behavioral Isolation occurs when animals have contradictory behaviors that prevent them from competing with each other.

10

In an ecosystem, mushrooms work as decomposers to break down dead organic matter and return vital nutrients to the soil.

How do mushrooms obtain nutrients?

A) Hyphae organize into structures from time to time that grows toward sunlight and produces nutrients by photosynthesis.

B) Large food particles are engulfed by the cells in the hyphae, forming food vacuoles that fuse with lysosomes to break down the particles through digestive enzymes.

C) The hyphae secrete enzymes that break down large molecules in the immediate environment, and then smaller particles are absorbed.

D) Hyphae forms tubes that transport food particles to specialized storage structures where the food is digested and the nutrients are absorbed.

11

Decomposers, such as many bacteria and fungi, are very important for any ecosystem because they recycle the dead organisms and waste into non-living elements so that plants can get the essesntial nutrients and and dead matter and waste do not pile up.

Which of the following about decomposers is not correct?

A) Decomposers are located at the base of the food chain.

B) In the nitrogen cycle, decomposers release ammonia from organic compounds.

C) Decomposers are nature's recyclers; they break down dead or decaying organisms.

D) Decomposers are heterotrophic; they get the energy from the organisms they consume.

12

Evolution occurs when the heritable differences become more common or rare, either non-randomly through natural selection or randomly through genetic drift.

Evolution of which of the followings is defined above?

A) Individuals
B) Organ systems
C) Living organisms
D) Populations

13

In photosynthesis, oxygen is created by splitting of which of the following?

A) Carbon monoxide
B) Water
C) Glucose
D) Carbon dioxide

14

Which of the following contributes to the occurrence of similar features in organisms from different phylogenetic?

A) Uniformitarianism
B) Convergent evolution
C) Stabilizing Section
D) Gradualism

15

The central dogma of molecular biology describes the two-step process, transcription and translation, by which the information in genes flows into proteins.

In the central dogma, which of the following is the most likely reason to why base pair mutation happens?

A) During replication, the DNA is inaccurately duplicated.
B) During meiosis, there is a failure in the separation of sister chromatids.
C) A small part of a chromosome is added to another chromosome.
D) A part of the chromosome breaks, flips and reinserts itself.

16

Wildlife corridors are critical for the maintenance of ecological processes.

Which of the following defines a wildlife corridor best?

A) It is a link of wildlife habitat, generally native vegetation, which joins two or larger areas of similar wildlife habitat.
B) An area that has been developed by humans, but where wildlife is still frequently seen.
C) A large, continuous area of undisturbed natural habitat.
D) A natural migration route of a population of animals.

17

Alleles can be dominant or recessive. When an individual has two of the same allele, whether dominant or recessive, they are homozygous.

What is true about homozygous individuals?

A) They have the same features.
B) They have two different alleles.
C) They are of the same species.
D) They have a pair of identical alleles.

18

The Endosymbiotic Theory was first proposed by former Boston University Biologist Lynn Margulis in the 1960's and officially in her 1981 book "Symbiosis in Cell Evolution".

Which of the following does The Endosymbiotic Theory state?

A) Eukaryotes originated from prokaryotes
B) Life arose from inorganic compounds
C) Prokaryotes originated from eukaryotes
D) The evolution of animals happened in close relationships with each other

19

Natural Selection is a key mechanism of evolution to explain how the diversity of life with so many species and large variations in characters came to exist. It was first formulated by Charles Darwin

Which of the following best describes Natural Selection?

A) Populations change over time.
B) Mutations occur in a random fashion.
C) Variations in populations are a survival advantage.
D) The environment determines which individuals will survive and reproduce.

20

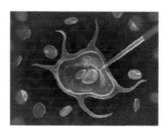

Genetic engineering, also called genetic modification, is the direct manipulation of an organism's genome using biotechnology. It is a set of technologies used to change the genetic makeup of cells, including the transfer of genes within and across species boundaries to produce improved or novel organisms.

Which of the following is a genetic engineering advancement in the medical field?

A) Gene therapy
B) Pesticides
C) Viruses
D) Good bacteria

21

Ecological efficiency is the efficiency with which energy can move from one trophic level to the one above.

Which of the following trophic levels has the highest ecological efficiency?

A) Secondary consumers
B) Producers
C) Decomposers
D) Tertiary consumers

22

Which of the following helps the transfer of the segments of DNA from the DNA of one organism to another?

A) Bacterial plasmids
B) Chromosomes from frogs
C) Plant DNA
D) Viruses

23

Among the following, which would be considered as the strongest evidence of a relatively close evolutionary relationship between two species?

A) Ancestors' fossils of the two species are found in the same geographic area.
B) Both species utilize the same 20 amino acids to form peptides and proteins.
C) Both species live in the same niches in their respective ecological communities.
D) Both embryos of the two species look almost very similar until the late stages of development.

24

The variety and variability of life on Earth is referred to as **Biodiversity**. It comprises living organisms from all sources.

Which of the following is not a part of biodiversity?

A) Plants
B) Microorganisms
C) Rocks and Minerals
D) Ecosystems

CONTINUE ▶

25

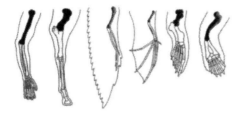

Which of the following reasons will most likely result in the similarity of design in the mammalian appendages shown above?

A) Common ancestry
B) Evolutionary convergence
C) Geographic isolation
D) Directional selection

26

A group of scientists observed that there is a decreased fertility in various aquatic animals like fish, reptiles, and insects in waterways near urbanized or agricultural areas.

Which of the following is most likely the cause of the decreased fertility rate?

A) There is a decline in the quantity and quality of food resources needed to sustain reproduction.
B) There is an interruption of mating behaviors and the destruction of breeding sites caused by human activity.
C) There is an increase in the number of invasive species present in degraded habitats.
D) There is a disruption of endocrine systems caused by the introduction of natural hormones and synthetic compounds.

Eutrophication is the process by which a body of water becomes enriched in dissolved nutrients (such as phosphates) that stimulate the growth of aquatic plant life usually resulting in the depletion of dissolved oxygen.

How is it possible to conclude that eutrophication of bodies of water has occurred?

A) By testing for the level of water acidity
B) By having greater species diversity in the water massive algae blooms
C) By having a vibrant, productive aquatic ecosystem
D) By having massive algae blooms

Which of the following definition is not correct?

A) Niche is the role that is played by a particular species in an ecosystem.
B) Habitat is the place where an organism or a biological population normally lives.
C) An ecosystem is a system that includes all living organisms (biotic factors) in an area.
D) A population is the number of organisms of the same species that live in a particular geographic area at the same time, with the capability of interbreeding.

29

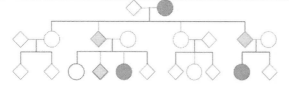

KEY
- ● Affected Male
- ◆ Affected Female
- ○ Unaffected Male
- ◇ Unaffected Female

A pedigree is a diagram that shows relationships between family members and patterns of inheritance for certain traits and diseases. The given pedigree above shows the sex-linked inheritance pattern of a gene.

What does the diagram show about the allele based on the pattern of inheritance?

A) The allele is X-linked recessive.
B) The allele is X-linked dominant.
C) The allele is Y-linked recessive.
D) The allele is Y-linked dominant.

30

A sea anemone uses its tentacles to protect a clownfish. In return, the anemone takes uneaten food from the clownfish.

Which of the following symbiotic relationships is given above?

A) Mutualism
B) Competition
C) Parasitism
D) Commensalisms

31

In biology, a **population** is all the organisms of the same group or species, which live in a particular geographical area, and have the capability of interbreeding.

Which of the density-independent factors given below does not affect a population?

A) Water supply
B) Rainfall
C) Soil nutrients
D) Predation

32

Protein synthesis is one of the most fundamental biological processes by which individual cells build their specific proteins. Both deoxyribonucleic acid (DNA) and ribonucleic acids (RNA) are involved in the process.

In protein synthesis which of the following carries amino acids to the ribosome.

A) Messenger RNA
B) Ribosomal RNA
C) DNA
D) Transfer RNA

33

Weathering is the breaking down of rocks and minerals on the surface of the Earth.

How do lichens, plant roots, and fungi are able to weather rock chemically?

A) By drawing molecular water from the crystals that make up the rock
B) By producing acids that cause the decomposition of the rock
C) By extracting minerals directly from the rock through osmosis
D) By manufacturing salts that alter the rock's crystal structure

34

Through molecular biology, a revolution in vaccine development has started.

Which of the following innovations in this field has contributed to the most recent changes in vaccine development?

A) Synthesis of vaccines made up of viral coat proteins which trigger immune responses.
B) Production of vaccines containing live pathogenic agents
C) Vaccines that provide lifelong immunity had been created.
D) Manufacturing of vaccines that allow transmission of lifelong immunity from one generation to the following generation.

35

It is the condition of a species (or another taxon) that ceases to exist in the chosen geographic area of study, though it still exists elsewhere. Local extinctions are contrasted with global extinctions.

Many crocodilian species have experienced extirpation, particularly the saltwater crocodile (Crocodylus porosus), which has been extirpated from Vietnam, Thailand, Java, and many other areas.

Which of the following is explained above?

A) Local extinction
B) Niche differentiation
C) Natural selection
D) Coevolution

36

Which of the following best defines population in a particular area?

A) All living organisms
B) All members of the same species
C) All living and nonliving organisms
D) All living things with their physical environment

37

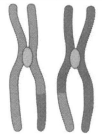

Synapsis is the process of pairing of two homologous chromosomes.

In synapsis, which of the following refers to the exchange of genes between homologous chromosomes?

A) Test cross
B) Polyploidy
C) Crossing-over
D) Homologous chromatids

38

Species is the principal natural taxonomic unit, ranking below a genus and denoted by a Latin binomial, e.g., Homo sapiens.

Which of the following is true about the members of the same species?

A) They look similar.
B) They are never aged.
C) They live in the same habitat.
D) They reproduce successfully within their group.

39

Which of the following defines any type of change which influences the sequence of bases in a gene?

A) Polyploid
B) Duplication
C) Mutation
D) Deletion

CONTINUE ▶

40

A food web is a natural interconnection of food chains and a graphical representation of what-eats-what in an ecological community.

In a food web, which of the following about the consumers is true?

A) They form the base of the trophic pyramid.
B) They make their own food.
C) They exhibit a heterotrophic mode of nutrition.
D) They get their energy directly from the Sun.

41

The percentage of cells in a sample that is in each of the five phases of replication – interphase, prophase, metaphase, anaphase, telophase – was analyzed by a biologist.

If the total of all the cells counted was 73 and 19 of the cells came from the telophase, what is the percentage of cells in the telophase?

A) 39%
B) 35%
C) 26%
D) 23%

CONTINUE ▶

42

Which of the following is the adjustment or changes in behavior, physiology, and structure of an organism to become more suited to the environment?

A) Homology
B) Analogy
C) Equilibrium
D) Adaptation

43

In which of the following ways natural selection would most likely affect the population of zebras that live on a savanna?

A) A considerable decrease in the mutation rate within the population.
B) A gradual decrease in the number of nonadaptive traits within the population.
C) A significant increase in the level of genetic variation within the population.
D) A substantial increase in the number of individuals in the population.

44

In biology and genealogy, the common ancestor is the ancestor that two or more descendants have in common.

Which of the following information provides with the strongest evidence that two different species share a common ancestor?

A) Similar functions of their appendages and organs
B) Their similarity in habitats and ecological niches
C) Their similar mating behaviors and rearing practices
D) The similarity in the structure of their genetic material and proteins

45

The fur on an polar bear appears white all year.

This is an example of which of the following?

A) It is a modification helping polar bear exchanging materials with its environment.
B) It is a metabolism regulating polar bear's activities.
C) It is example of responding to internal stimuli.
D) It is an adaptation helping polar bear to survive.

46

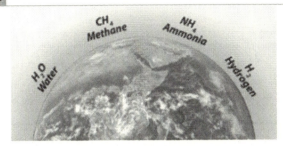

For decades, scientists believed that the atmosphere of early Earth was highly reduced.

Which of the following gas does not make up the primitive atmosphere?

A) Hydrogen
B) Ammonia
C) Oxygen
D) Water vapour

47

In DNA, bases are bonded with hydrogen bonds. Cytosine pairs with _____ while Adenine bonds with _____.

Which of the following pairs fill in the empty space in the above sentence?

A) Guanine/Thymine
B) Cytosine/Adenine
C) Guanine/Thymine
D) Adenine/Cytosine

48

In the cycle of carbon in the Earth's ecosystems, carbon dioxide is fixed by photosynthetic organisms to form organic nutrients and is ultimately restored to the inorganic state by respiration, protoplasmic decay, or combustion.

Which of the following is not true of the carbon cycle?

A) Carbon dioxide (CO_2) is fixed by glycosylation.
B) 10% of all available carbon (C) is in the air.
C) Plants fix carbon (C) in the form of glucose.
D) Animals release carbon through respiration.

CONTINUE ▶

49

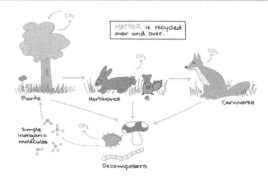

An ecosystem is a community of living organisms in conjunction with the nonliving components of their environment interacting as a system.

Which type of ecosystem occupies the most acreage in the United States?

A) Cultivated land
B) Wetland
C) Forest land
D) Urban land

50

DNA is deoxyribonucleic acid, a self-replicating material which is present in nearly all living organisms as the main constituent of chromosomes. It is the carrier of genetic information.

Which of the following terms about DNA replication process is not defined correctly?

A) Nucleotide is the long chain of amino acids that is created during translation.
B) Transcription is the process in which a cell's DNA is copied into messenger RNA.
C) Translation is the process in which a cell converts genetic information carried in an mRNA molecule into a protein.
D) Replication is the process in which a cell's DNA is copied prior to cellular reproduction.

51

What is the name of small rounded piece of DNA which contains accessory DNA?

A) Messenger RNA
B) Transfer DNA
C) Mitochondrial DNA
D) Plasmid

52

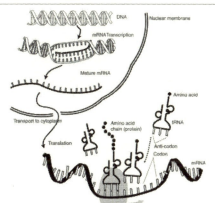

X: Transcription

Y: Translation

Z: Replication

Protein synthesis is the process whereby cells generate new proteins. It includes the steps given above.

Which of the following is the correct order in the protein synthesis?

A) X, then Z
B) Y, then X
C) Z, then Y
D) X, then Y

53

The Hardy - Weinberg principle, also known as the Hardy - Weinberg equilibrium states that allele and genotype frequencies in a population will remain constant from generation to generation in the absence of other evolutionary influences.

Which of the following factors will affect the Hardy-Weinberg law of equilibrium, leading to evolutionary change?

A) No mutations
B) No immigration
C) Large population
D) Non-random mating

54

Which of the following is the duplication of genetic material into another cell?

A) Replication
B) Division
C) Cloning
D) Cell duplication

55

Primary succession is one of two types of the biological and ecological succession of plant life.

When does Primary succession occur?

A) After a forest fire
B) Before a housing development is built
C) After the soil is incapable of sustaining life
D) Before nutrient enrichment

56

Which of the following is the hypothesis that evolution proceeds chiefly by the accumulation of slow changes (in contrast to the punctuationist model)?

A) Mass extinction
B) Status
C) Catastrophism
D) Gradualism

57

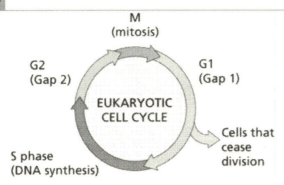

Which of the following describes how gene replication occurs in an eukaryotic cell before the cell division?

A) An amino acid is attached to a new strand of DNA by a DNA polymerase.
B) Two separate strands of DNA are added with nucleotide base pairs.
C) Complementary pairs are formed by strands of mRNA transcribed from DNA.
D) During the early phase of meiosis, chromosomes are separated into two strands of RNA.

58

Which of the following about the reproduction of viruses is not correct?

A) Lysogeny is the process by which a virus incorporates its genetic material into the genome of its host cell.
B) The Lytic cycle is common to both animal viruses and bacterial phages. The lytic cycle results in the destruction of the infected cell and its membrane.
C) A bacteriophage virus infects a bacteria by injecting its DNA into the bacterial cytoplasm, or liquid space inside of the cell wall.
D) One key difference between the lytic cycle and the lysogenic cycle is that the lytic cycle does not lyse the host cell straight away.

59

Reproductive isolation refers to the situation where different species may live in the same area, but the properties of individuals prevent them from interbreeding. The things which stop species or groups of organisms reproducing sexually are called isolating mechanisms.

What is not true about reproductive isolation?

A) Populations can not exchange genes.
B) It can occur by preventing fertilization.
C) It can result in speciation.
D) It is not a phenomenon of species living on islands.

60

Evolution is a theory about the origin of life. It is the process by which organisms change over time as a result of changes in heritable physical or behavioral traits.

Which of the following does not support the evolution?

A) Analogous structures
B) Comparative anatomy
C) Organic chemistry
D) Comparison of DNA among organisms

61

DNA replication is the process of copying the DNA within the cells. This process involves RNA, DNA, and several enzymes. There are three steps in the process of DNA replication.

In which of the following the steps DNA duplication is given in the correct order?

A) Elongation, termination, initiation
B) Initiation, elongation, termination
C) Termination elongation, initiation
D) Elongation, initiation, termination

A remarkable lack of genetic diversity has been noticed in the population by researchers studying northern elephant seals. In contrast, a normal amount of genetic variation is observed in the southern elephant seal population.

Which of the following explains the difference in the two elephant seal populations the best?

A) There was a great reduction in the northern elephant seal population in the recent past, while there wasn't any in the southern elephant seal population.
B) Northern elephant seals rival with many other seal species, while southern elephant seals have no close rivals.
C) Southern elephant seals mate basically inside their own group, while northern elephant seals mate mainly outside their own group.
D) A lot of mutagenic substances from pollution affect southern elephant seals negatively, while northern elephant seals live in less polluted waters.

Abiotic factor is a nonliving condition or thing, as climate or habitat, which influences or affects an ecosystem and the organisms in it. Abiotic factors can determine which species of organisms will survive in a given environment.

Which of the following is not an abiotic factor?

A) Rainfall
B) Soil quality
C) Temperature
D) Bacteria

64

The food chain shows how each living thing gets food. It also shows how nutrients and energy are passed from creature to creature. Food chains begin with plant-life and end with animal-life.

Which of the following eats secondary consumers?

A) Decomposers
B) Tertiary consumers
C) Cyanobacteria
D) Primary consumers

65

Greenhouse Gases in the atmosphere absorb and emit radiation within the thermal infrared range. Some of the Greenhouse Gases are water vapor, carbon dioxide, nitrous oxide, etc.

Which of the following is also a greenhouse gas?

A) Propane
B) Methane
C) Helium
D) Butane

66

Which of the following is characterized by the stage depicted in the above diagram where a genetic material is attached to spindle fibers followed by nuclear membrane breakdown?

A) The assortment of chromosomes to form haploid cells in meiosis
B) The separation of sister chromatids in mitosis
C) Crossing over during mitosis
D) Nondisjunction of at least one pair of sister chromatids during meiosis

67

A **gene** is a sequence of DNA that contains genetic information and can influence the phenotype of an organism. Within a gene, the sequence of bases along a DNA strand defines a messenger RNA sequence, which then defines one or more protein sequences.

If a DNA strand has the base sequence of TCAGTA, which of the following DNA complement sequence would it have?

A) ATGACT
B) AGTCAT
C) TCAGTA
D) AGUCAU

68

Which of the following parameter is the most common factor that limits the growth of plants in terrestrial ecosystems?

A) The moisture level of the soil
B) The level of carbon dioxide in the atmosphere
C) The level of carbonates in the soil
D) The nitrogen level in the atmosphere

69

Which of the stages given below was not a stage in the origin of life?

A) The origin of biological monomers
B) The origin of protein synthesis
C) The origin of biological polymers
D) The evolution from molecules to cells

70

It describes changes in population genetics in which extreme values for a trait are favored over intermediate values. In this case, the variance of the trait increases and the population is divided into two distinct groups.

Which of the following is explained in the above paragraph?

A) Disruptive selection
B) Directional selection
C) Heterozygote advantage
D) Directional selection

71

Which of the following is the independent variable in an experiment which measures the growth of bacteria at different temperatures?

A) Intensity of light
B) Temperature
C) The growth of the number of colonies
D) Type of the bacteria used

72

Acid rain is caused by emissions of sulfur dioxide and nitrogen oxide, which react with the water molecules in the atmosphere to produce acids.

Which of the following about the acid rains is not correct?

A) When sulfurous gases such as sulfur dioxide (SO2) react with water they produce ammonia.

B) Scientific evidence has linked acid rain to decreased fish and wildlife populations, degraded lakes and streams, and human health hazards.

C) Acid rain became a household term in the 1980s when unchecked emissions from industry and motor vehicles were blamed for causing environmental deterioration.

D) Acid rain is a result of air pollution because sulfur dioxide and nitrogen oxides are bi-products from burning fuels in electric utilities and from other industrial and natural sources.

73

Natural selection is one of the basic mechanisms of evolution. According to Darwin's theory of natural selection, organisms which are better adapted to their environment tend to survive and produce more offspring.

Which of the following is true about natural selection?

A) It acts on the genotype.
B) It does not happen instantly.
C) It is a phenomenon of plants only.
D) It acts on the phenotype.

74

Which of the following enzymes unwind DNA during the replication process?

A) Replicase
B) Topoisomerases
C) Helicase
D) DNAse

75

It is an example of an organ or bone that appears in different animals, underlining anatomical commonalities demonstrating descent from a common ancestor.

Which of the following is explained in the paragraph given above?

A) Polymorphic structures
B) Homologous structures
C) Vestigial structures
D) Analogous structures

76

The **water cycle** describes how water evaporates from the surface of the earth, rises into the atmosphere, cools and condenses into rain or snow in clouds, and falls again to the surface as precipitation.

Which of the following terms is not associated with the water cycle?

A) Precipitation
B) Transpiration
C) Evaporation
D) Fixation

77

Which of the following processes contributes most to the big variety of living things throughout the world?

A) Meiosis
B) Alternation of generations
C) Sexual reproduction
D) Mitosis

Natural selection is one of the basic mechanisms of evolution through which populations of living organisms can adapt and change.

Artificial selection, also called "selective breeding", is where humans select for desirable traits in agricultural products or animals

Which of the following is not true about natural and artificial selection?

A) Natural selection has been developed by Charles Darwin first during the 1830's.
B) Natural selection is performed on all types of organisms, whereas artificial selection is processed on some selective organisms of humans desires.
C) Natural selection is a slow and long process, whereas artificial selection is faster.
D) Natural selection selects required character, whereas artificial selection selects adaptable character.

The theory of evolution by natural selection is the process by which organisms change over time as a result of changes in heritable physical or behavioral traits.

Which of the principles given below is NOT a part of Darwin's theory of evolution?

A) An individual has the ability to evolve.
B) Individuals with different genotypes make up a population.
C) Some traits give an individual a better chance to survive.
D) Traits can be inherited.

80

Biological diversity means the variability among living organisms from all sources including, inter alia, terrestrial, marine and other aquatic ecosystems. Diversity can be within species, between species, and of ecosystems.

Which of the following is not true of diversity?

A) Skeletons of organisms are similar to allow for diversity
B) There would be extinction if there was no diversity
C) Diversity is increasing all the time
D) Fossil evidence supports diversity

81

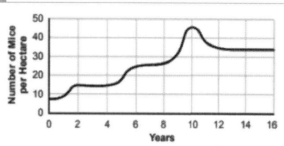

Based on the graph above that illustrates change over time in a population of nonnative mice in a forest, what is the approximate number of the ecosystem's carrying capacity for the mouse population?

A) 15 mice per hectare.
B) 25 mice per hectare.
C) 35 mice per hectare.
D) 45 mice per hectare.

82

Some bacteria transfer genetic material to another through direct contact. During this process, one bacterium serves as the donor of the genetic material, and the other serves as the recipient. It provides the recipient bacterium with some sort of genetic advantage.

What is the special name of this kind of DNA transfer between bacteria?

A) Binary fission
B) Translation
C) Transformation
D) Conjugation

83

dichlorodiphenyltrichloroethane

Environmental toxins can accumulate to high levels in organisms at the top of the food chain. If DDT is present in an ecosystem, in which of the following organisms will the DDT concentration be highest?

A) Frog
B) Eagle
C) Grasshopper
D) Crabgrass

84

The **codon** is a nucleotide triplet that encodes an amino acid. Each group of three nucleotides encodes one amino acid.

A protein is sixty amino acids in length. How many nucleotides are required to code this DNA sequence?

A) 20
B) 30
C) 180
D) 360

85

The DNA molecule consists of two chains that spiral around an imaginary axis to form a double helix (spiral.)

Which area of a DNA nucleotide can vary?

A) Deoxyribose
B) Five carbon sugar
C) Nitrogenous base
D) A phosphorus atom surrounded by four oxygen atoms

86

Evolution proceeds chiefly by the accumulation of slow changes.

Which evolutionary theory did Darwin support?

A) Punctualism
B) Equilibrium
C) Convergence
D) Gradualism

87

Decomposers are organisms that break down dead or decaying bodies. They are essential for any ecosystem. If they weren't in the ecosystem, the plants would not get crucial nutrients, and dead matter and waste would pile up.

Which of the following is not correct about decomposers?

A) Phosphorous is added back to the soil by decomposers.
B) Ammonification is the formation of ammonia or its compounds by decomposition of organic matter.
C) Decomposers can help recycle the Carbon accumulated in the organic material.
D) Decomposers belong to the Genus Escherichia.

88

A fundamental concept in ecology is the **competitive exclusion** principle which states that two species with similar ecological niches cannot exist in the same environment. One will always out-compete the other.

Which of the following about the competition is not correct?

A) Competition is a struggle, a fight, two livings opposing each other to survive.
B) Organisms compete for the resources they need to survive; air, water, food, and space.
C) Competition happens when two livings want the same thing, but there isn't enough of it to go around.
D) Competition in the natural world is eminent, and it always happens in the same way.

89

Competition in biology is a term that refers to the rivalry between or among living things for territory, resources, goods, mates, etc.

In the competition between organisms, which of the following is most generally true?

A) When resources are not sufficient, native species typically pish out non-native species.
B) Resource partitioning is more characteristic of animal species than of plant species.
C) There is a more intense competition between members of the same species than members of different species.
D) Competition is more likely to happen between species that occupy the same niche than species in different niches.

90

What is the basis for the acceptance of James Watson and Francis Crick's three-dimensional model of the DNA molecule?

A) Its ability to explain the mechanism of DNA replication and its integration with existing evidence on genetics.
B) The collected data, before their research was begun, about the use of DNA molecule.
C) Analysis of the DNA molecule through the use of state-of-the-art technology.
D) Its ability to explain the roles of enzyme in DNA transcription and the quality of the researcher's published work.

91

Photosynthesis and respiration are complementary reactions within the environment. They are the same reactions but occurring in reverse.

In the comparison of respiration to photosynthesis, which statement is correct?

A) Glucose is produced in respiration but not in photosynthesis.
B) Oxygen is a waste product in photosynthesis but not in respiration.
C) Carbon dioxide is formed in photosynthesis but not in respiration.
D) Water is used in respiration but not in photosynthesis.

92

The body fluids in saltwater fish are lower in salinity than their salty marine habitat. It allows them to counteract the osmotic pressure exerted by the minerals dissolved in the water.

Which of the following is prevented by these fluids?

A) Loss of too many minerals from the tissues
B) Loss of too much water from the tissues
C) Absorption of too much water into the tissues
D) Absorption of too many minerals into the tissues

93

Gene structure is the organization of specialized sequence elements within a gene.

Which of the following molecules specify the structure of Genes?

A) Cholesterol
B) Lipids
C) Proteins
D) Nucleic acids

94

Biological diversity means the variability among living organisms from all sources, It can be within species, between species and ecosystems.

How does diversity aid a population?

A) Add improvements to the population.
B) Mates are attracted to a diverse population.
C) Potential mates like conformity.
D) It varies the DNA differences in the population.

95

If a population is in Hardy-Weinberg equilibrium and the frequency of the recessive allele is 0.2, what percentage of the population would be expected to be heterozygous?

A) 4%
B) 16%
C) 32%
D) 64%

96

Ecosystems maintain themselves by cycling energy and nutrients obtained from external sources.

Which of the following is correct about the flow of energy in an ecosystem?

A) Chemical energy is converted into radiant energy, which is then converted into chemical energy at the next trophic level
B) Smaller organisms need less energy per gram of body weight than do larger organisms
C) Energy flow between trophic levels is inefficient because energy is lost when one trophic level goes to a level higher.
D) Energy transfer between organisms normally involves conservation of heat energy

CONTINUE ▶

SECTION 5 - ECOLOGY & EVOLUTION & GENETICS

#	Answer	Topic	Subtopic	#	Answer	Topic	Subtopic	#	Answer	Topic	Subtopic	#	Answer	Topic	Subtopic
1	C	TNESBD	SNESBD1	25	A	TNESBB	SNESBB1	49	C	TNESBD	SNESBD1	73	D	TNESBB	SNESBB2
2	B	TNESBD	SNESBD1	26	D	TNESBD	SNESBD2	50	A	TNESBC	SNESBC1	74	C	TNESBC	SNESBC1
3	D	TNESBD	SNESBD1	27	D	TNESBD	SNESBD2	51	D	TNESBC	SNESBC1	75	B	TNESBB	SNESBB1
4	B	TNESBB	SNESBB1	28	C	TNESBD	SNESBD2	52	D	TNESBC	SNESBC1	76	D	TNESBD	SNESBD1
5	A	TNESBD	SNESBD2	29	B	TNESBC	SNESBC1	53	D	TNESBB	SNESBB1	77	A	TNESBB	SNESBB2
6	A	TNESBB	SNESBB1	30	A	TNESBD	SNESBD1	54	C	TNESBC	SNESBC1	78	D	TNESBB	SNESBB2
7	D	TNESBB	SNESBB1	31	D	TNESBD	SNESBD2	55	C	TNESBB	SNESBB2	79	A	TNESBB	SNESBB1
8	B	TNESBD	SNESBD1	32	D	TNESBC	SNESBC1	56	D	TNESBB	SNESBB1	80	A	TNESBB	SNESBB2
9	B	TPRXSAB	SPRXSAB2	33	B	TNESBD	SNESBD1	57	B	TNESBC	SNESBC1	81	C	TNESBD	SNESBD2
10	C	TNESBD	SNESBD1	34	A	TNESBC	SNESBC2	58	D	TNESBD	SNESBD1	82	D	TNESBC	SNESBC1
11	A	TNESBD	SNESBD1	35	A	TNESBD	SNESBD2	59	D	TNESBB	SNESBB2	83	B	TNESBD	SNESBD2
12	D	TNESBB	SNESBB2	36	B	TNESBD	SNESBD2	60	C	TNESBB	SNESBB2	84	C	TNESBC	SNESBC1
13	B	TNESBD	SNESBD1	37	C	TNESBC	SNESBC1	61	B	TNESBC	SNESBC1	85	C	TNESBC	SNESBC1
14	B	TNESBB	SNESBB1	38	D	TNESBB	SNESBB1	62	A	TNESBB	SNESBB1	86	D	TNESBB	SNESBB2
15	A	TNESBC	SNESBC1	39	C	TNESBC	SNESBC1	63	D	TNESBB	SNESBB2	87	D	TNESBD	SNESBD1
16	A	TNESBD	SNESBD2	40	C	TNESBD	SNESBD1	64	B	TNESBD	SNESBD1	88	D	TNESBB	SNESBB2
17	D	TNESBC	SNESBC1	41	C	TNESBC	SNESBC1	65	B	TNESBD	SNESBD1	89	D	TNESBD	SNESBD2
18	A	TNESBB	SNESBB2	42	D	TNESBB	SNESBB1	66	B	TNESBC	SNESBC1	90	A	TNESBC	SNESBC1
19	D	TNESBB	SNESBB1	43	B	TNESBD	SNESBD2	67	B	TNESBC	SNESBC1	91	B	TNESBD	SNESBD1
20	A	TNESBC	SNESBC2	44	D	TNESBB	SNESBB2	68	A	TNESBD	SNESBD1	92	B	TNESBD	SNESBD2
21	B	TNESBD	SNESBD1	45	D	TNESBB	SNESBB1	69	B	TNESBB	SNESBB2	93	C	TNESBC	SNESBC1
22	A	TNESBC	SNESBC1	46	C	TNESBD	SNESBD1	70	A	TNESBB	SNESBB1	94	A	TNESBB	SNESBB2
23	D	TNESBB	SNESBB2	47	A	TNESBC	SNESBC1	71	B	TNESBD	SNESBD1	95	C	TNESBB	SNESBB1
24	C	TNESBD	SNESBD2	48	A	TNESBD	SNESBD1	72	A	TNESBD	SNESBD1	96	C	TNESBD	SNESBD1

Topics & Subtopics

Code	Description	Code	Description
SNESBB	Evolution	SNESBD	Ecology
SNESBB1	Evolutionary Patterns	SNESBD1	Ecosystems
SNESBB2	History & Origin of Life	SNESBD2	Biodiversity
SNESBC	Genetics	SPRXSAB	Science
SNESBC1	Inheritance	SPRXSAB2	Basic Science
SNESBC2	Biotechnology		

TEST DIRECTION

DIRECTIONS

Read the questions carefully and then choose the ONE best answer to each question.

Be sure to allocate your time carefully so you are able to complete the entire test within the testing session. You may go back and review your answers at any time.

You may use any available space in your test booklet for scratch work.

Questions in this booklet are not actual test questions but they are the samples for commonly asked questions.

This test aims to cover all topics which may appear on the actual test. However some topics may not be covered.

Studying this booklet will be preparing you for the actual test. It will not guarantee improving your test score but it will help you pass your exam on the first attempt.

Some useful tips for answering multiple choice questions;

- Start with the questions that you can easily answer.

- Underline the keywords in the question.

- Be sure to read all the choices given.

- Watch for keywords such as NOT, always, only, all, never, completely.

- Do not forget to answer every question.

1

Waves traveling through a solid medium can be either transverse waves or longitudinal waves.

Which of the following about the waves is not correct?

A) The longitudinal and transverse waves are two dimensional.
B) Water waves, guitar and other strings are examples of transverse waves.
C) A longitudinal waves is a wave where the movement of the medium is in the same direction as the wave.
D) A transverse wave is a wave in which particles of the medium move in a direction perpendicular to the direction which the wave moves.

2

A group of people on the planet Mars are having a tug-of-war. They have a 20 kg box with ropes tied to either side. Four of the people pull to the right with a total force of 270 N and four of the people pull to the left with a total force of 170 N. If the acceleration of gravity on Mars is 3.8 m/s², which of the following is not correct?

A) The weight of the box is 76 N
B) The normal force on the box is 76 N
C) The net force acting on the box is 100 N
D) The acceleration of the box is 3.8 meter per second square.

3

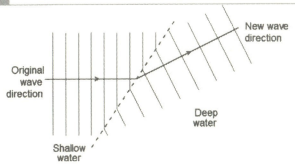

When a wave moves from shallow water to deep water, how do the frequency, speed, and the wavelength change?

A) The wavelength increases, frequency decreases, and the speed increases.
B) The wavelength decreases, frequency does not change, and the speed decreases.
C) The wavelength increases, frequency does not change, and the speed increases.
D) The wavelength increases, frequency does not change, and the speed decreases.

4

If you increase the speed of an object by 10%, then how many percent will its kinetic energy increase?

A) 10
B) 20
C) 21
D) 40

5

The quantity is either a vector or a scalar. Scalars are the quantities that are fully described by only magnitude. Vectors are the quantities that are fully described by both a magnitude and a direction.

Which of the following is a vector quantity?

A) Mass
B) Speed
C) Distance
D) Displacement

6

Ethan runs halfway around a circular path of radius 40 m in 5 seconds. What is the displacement of Ethan?

A) 20 m
B) 40 m
C) 60 m
D) 80 m

7

If the speed of an object is doubled, how does its kinetic energy change?

A) It decreases.
B) It doubles.
C) It quadruples.
D) It stays same.

8

A 50-kilogram rock rolls off the edge of a cliff. If it is traveling at a speed of 12 m/s when it hits the ground, what is the height of the cliff? (g = 10 m/s²)

A) 4.16 m
B) 7.2 m
C) 12 m
D) 14.4 m

9

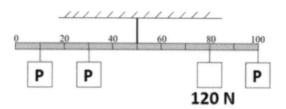

The weight of the uniform rod given above is 30N.

If the rod is at equillibrium, not rotating, what is the weight of P?

A) 50 N
B) 120 N
C) 160 N
D) 360 N

10

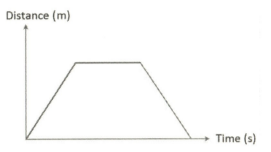

Which of the following about the distance-time graph given above is not correct?

A) The area under distance-time graph gives displacement.
B) Horizontal line in a distance-time graph means object is not moving.
C) Slope of distance-time graph gives velocity. Steeper line indicates a larger distance moved in a given time; in other words, higher speed.
D) If both time and distance are increasing constantly, then the object may be moving at a constant speed.

11

A pickup truck is being driven on the highway. It starts raining and rain begins filling up the back of the truck. If the driver maintains the same velocity, and the road stays flat and level, how does the momentum of the truck change, and which law applies to this situation?

A) Momentum Decreases; Conservation of Momentum
B) Momentum increases; Conservation of Momentum
C) Momentum decreases; Conservation of Kinetic Energy
D) Momentum increases; Conservation of Kinetic Energy

12

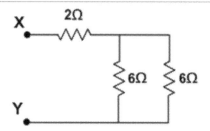

If the potential difference between the points X and Y in the circuit given above is 140V, what is the current passing through 2 ohm resistor?

A) 5 A
B) 10 A
C) 28 A
D) 70 A

13

Which of the following about heat is not correct?

A) Heat is the transfer of energy from one object to another due to a difference in temperature.
B) Heat needed to raise the temperature by 1 Celcius degree is called the specific heat capacity.
C) The latent heat associated with melting a solid or freezing a liquid is called the heat of fusion.
D) In thermodynamics, heat is energy in transfer to or from a thermodynamic system. The standard unit of heat in SI is the Celcius degree.

14

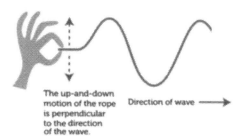

The up-and-down motion of the rope is perpendicular to the direction of the wave. Direction of wave →

What kind of a wave is given above?

A) Compressional wave
B) Longitudinal wave
C) Transverse wave
D) Pressure wave

15

Two cars are traveling in the same direction. The distance between the cars is 120m and their velocities are 2m/s and 6m/s. How many seconds later will the faster car catch the slower car if the fast moving car is behind the slower car?

A) 15
B) 20
C) 30
D) 40

16

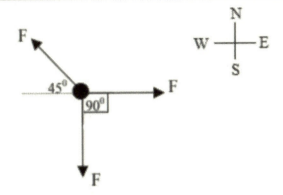

In the figure given above, three forces of equal magnitude F act on an object. Which of the following about the motion of the object is true?

A) It will be at rest.
B) It will accelerate towards north-west.
C) It will accelerate towards south-east.
D) It will accelerate towards north-east.

17

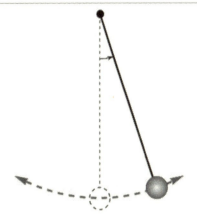

A pendulum is a weight suspended from a pivot so that it can swing freely.

If a pendlum has a period of 5 seconds, then what is its frequency?

A) 0.2 Hz
B) 1 Hz
C) 5 Hz
D) 25 Hz

18

A resistor is a circuit element that limits or regulates the flow of electrical current in an electric circuit.

Which of the following about adding a resistor to an electric circuit is not correct?

A) It does not affect the current of the circuit.
B) It does not affect the potential difference of the circuit.
C) It decreases the total resistance of the circuit if resistor is connected in parallel with the other resistors of the circuit.
D) It increases the total resistance of the circuit if resistor is connected in series with the other resistors of the circuit.

19

Two positive charges with magnitudes 4Q and Q are separated by a distance r. Which of the following statements about the electrical force between the charges is not true?

A) If you double both charges, then coulomb force will double.
B) The charge with a smaller magnitude exerts a smaller force on the bigger charge.
C) If you increase the distance between the charges, then coulomb force will increase.
D) The coulomb forces on each charge are the same in magnitude and opposite in direction.

20

I. The displacement is zero.

II. The distance is zero.

III. The average speed is zero.

IV. The average velocity is zero.

An object that is moving with constant speed travels twice around a circular path. Which of the following statements about this motion is (arc) correct?

A) I and III
B) I and IV
C) II and III
D) II and IV

21

Megan is standing on an icy pond in her ice skates. She needs to move to the east shore of the pond and is having trouble moving. She has a very heavy backpack in her arms and decides to throw it parallel to the ice.

Which direction should Megan throw her backpack to enable her to get closer to the east shore, and which law applies to this situation?

A) West; Conservation of Energy
B) East; Conservation of Energy
C) East; Conservation of Momentum
D) West; Conservation of Momentum

22

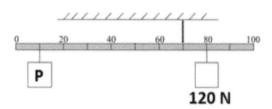

The uniform rod given in the figure above has a weight of 30N.

If the rod is not rotating, what is the weight of P?

A) 10 N
B) 90 N
C) 105 N
D) 120 N

23

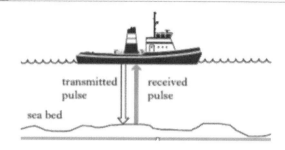

A ship given above sends sound waves to the sea bed, and receives the reflected waves to determine the depth.

If it takes 4 seconds to receive the transmitted pulse, how many meters is the depth of the sea bed? (The average speed of sound in seawater is about 1,500 meters per second)

A) 350 m
B) 3,000 m
C) 6,000 m
D) 12,000 m

24

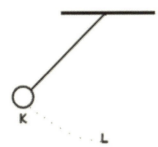

As the ball swings from K to L, which of the following is not correct? (Assume there is air friction)

A) Speed of the ball will increase.
B) Kinetic energy of the ball will increase.
C) Potential energy of the ball will decrease.
D) Mechanical energy of the ball will stay the same.

25

An object moving under the influence of the gravitational force –with no air resistance– is said to be in **free fall**. During each second of fall, the speed of the object increases by 10 m/s (more precisely, 9.8 m/s).

If a ball falls from a height of 80 m, approximately how many seconds will it take for the ball to hit the ground?

A) 4
B) 8
C) 16
D) 80

26

- Force is a push or a pull.

- Force of Gravity, in other words, weight, is the force between you and the Earth.

- The combination of all forces acting on an object is called the net force.

- The SI unit of force is Newton. Force is a vector quantity.

Some facts about force are given above. Which of the following about force is not true?

A) The net force acting on an object depends on the magnitudes and directions of the applied forces.
B) If the net force is zero, then the object is said to be in equilibrium, and the object does not move.
C) Tension may be described as the pulling force transmitted axially by the means of a string, cable, or a chain.
D) The normal force is the support force exerted upon an object that is in contact with another stable object.

27

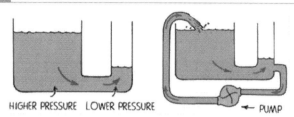

A simple hydraulic circuit is analogous to an electric circuit. What does the pump of hydraulic circuit represent for an electric circuit?

A) Wire
B) Battery
C) Lamp
D) Resistor

28

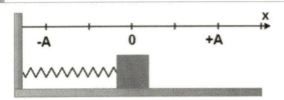

A mass attached to a spring given above is making simple harmonic motion between the points -A and +A.

Which of the following about the spring-mass system is not correct?

A) In the equation $F = -kx$, k represents for spring constant.
B) When the mass reaches point +A its instantaneous velocity is zero.
C) When the mass reaches point $x = 0$ its instantaneous acceleration is the maximum.
D) Elastic Potential Energy and Kinetic Energy are the two types of energy in a mass-spring system

29

According to Newton's third law, for every action force, there is a reaction force.

When you exert a force on an object, the object exerts a reaction force on you. Which of the following defines the reaction force?

A) Opposite in direction and equal in magnitude
B) In the same direction and equal in magnitude
C) Opposite in direction and greater in magnitude
D) In the same direction and weaker in magnitude

30

Which of the following about Newton's second law is correct?

A) Other name given to the second law is law of inertia.
B) An object will only accelerate if there is a net force acting upon it.
C) It is the tendency of an object in motion to remain in motion, or an object at rest to remain at rest unless acted upon by a force.
D) The acceleration of an object as produced by a net force is inversely proportional to the magnitude of the net force.

31

Under the influence of a force, an object of mass 4 kg accelerates from 2 m/s to 6 m/s in 4s. How much work is done on the object during this time?

A) 8 J
B) 32 J
C) 56 J
D) 64 J

32

Sebastian walks 4m East and 3m North. What is the distance and displacement of Sebastian?

A) Displacement is 7m, distance is 5m towards North of East.
B) Displacement is 7m, distance is 5m towards East of North.
C) Distance is 7m, displacement is 5m towards North of East.
D) Distance is 7m, displacement is 5m towards East of North.

33

An archer uses a bow to fire two similar arrows with the same force. One arrow is fired at an angle of 45 degrees with the horizontal and the other with an angle of 50 degrees with the horizontal.

If you neglect air resistance, which of the following about the projectile motion of the arrows is not correct?

A) The arrow fired at an angle of 50 degrees will have a longer flight time, and longer horizontal range.

B) The arrow fired at an angle of 45 degrees will have a shorter flight time, and longer horizontal range.

C) The arrow fired at an angle of 45 degrees will have a smaller vertical speed, and smaller maximum height.

D) The arrow fired at an angle of 50 degrees will have a bigger vertical speed, and bigger maximum height.

34

$$a = \frac{\Delta V}{\Delta t} = \frac{V_{final} - V_{initial}}{t_{final} - t_{initial}}$$

A car moving with a velocity of 20m/s speeds up to 80m/s in 5 seconds. How many metre per second squared (m/s^2) is the acceleration of the car?

A) 4
B) 12
C) 16
D) 20

CONTINUE ▶

35

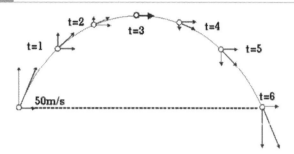

A ball is making projectile motion. Trajectory of the ball and initial horizontal velocity are given above. If you ignore air friction, what is the velocity of the ball when it is at the highest point? (g = 10 N/kg)

A) 20 m/s
B) 30 m/s
C) 40 m/s
D) 50 m/s

36

A man pushes a grocery cart which has a total mass of 40.0 kg. If the force of friction on the cart is 10.0 N, how hard does the man have to push so that the cart accelerates at 2.50 m/s²?

A) 16 N
B) 90 N
C) 100 N
D) 110 N

37

Which of the following about the circular motion is not correct?

A) In circular motion the velocity of the object is tangent to the circle.
B) In circular motion, the direction of the centripetal acceleration is outwards.
C) Period is the time for a complete rotation, and frequency is the number of rotations per unit time.
D) Uniform circular motion is an accelerated motion because the direction of the speed is changing.

38

A car and its acceleration is given above. If the initial speed of the car is 20 m/s, what will be its speed after 3 seconds?

A) 8 m/s
B) 12 m/s
C) 20 m/s
D) 32 m/s

39

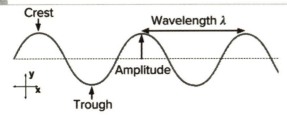

In physics, a wave is a disturbance that transfers energy through matter or space. Waves consist of oscillations or vibrations of a physical medium or a field, around relatively fixed locations and there is no transfer of mass.

Which of the following about the waves is not correct?

A) Wavelength is shown by Greek letter lambda, λ.
B) The amplitude is the maximum displacement from the equilibrium.
C) Velocity of a wave is calculated by multiplying wavelength with the period of the wave.
D) The wavelength is the distance between the top of one crest to the top of the next one.

40

A 10 Newton force and a 15 Newton force are acting on an object from a single point in opposite directions.

What additional force must be added to produce equilibrium?

A) 5 N acting in the same direction as the 10 N force
B) 5 N acting in the same direction as the 15 N force
C) 10 N acting in the same direction as the 10 N force
D) 25 N acting in the same direction as the 15 N force

41

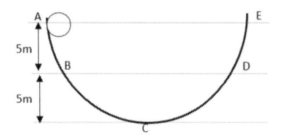

A ball having a mass of 8kg is released from the point A. If there is no friction, which of the following about the ball is not true? ($g = 10$ m/s^2)

A) Its potential energy at point A is 800J.
B) Its kinetic energy at point D is 400J.
C) Its velocity at point D is 100 m/s.
D) Its velocity at point C is 14.14 m/s.

42

A 4 Ω resistor and a 12 Ω resistor are connected in parallel to a 24 V source. What is the total current in the circuit?

A) 1.5 A
B) 2 A
C) 4 A
D) 8 A

43

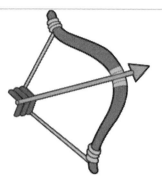

The archer places an arrow across the middle of the bow with the bowstring in the arrow's nock.

Which of the following is not correct?

A) The bow can do work on the arrow.
B) When a bow is drawn back, potential energy is stored in the bow.
C) Potential energy stored in the bow is gravitational potential energy.
D) When the arrow is released, potential energy stored in the bow will be converted into kinetic energy.

44

$$F_g = G\frac{m_1 \cdot m_2}{r^2} \qquad F_e = k\frac{q_1 \cdot q_2}{r^2}$$

Gravitational Attraction   Coulomb's Law

Which of the following is true when comparing the gravitational force and the electric force?

A) Both forces are always attractive.
B) Both forces increase in magnitude as the distance between the masses or charges increases.
C) Both forces are inversely proportional to the product of the masses or the charges.
D) Both forces are inversely proportional to the square of the distance between the masses or charges.

45

An electrical circuit is a path or line through which an electrical current flows.

Which of the following about the elements of a circiut is not correct?

A) Battery converts electric energy into chemical energy.
B) Resistors can convert electrical energy to heat.
C) Ammeter measures the current in a circuit.
D) Voltmeter measures electrical potential difference.

46

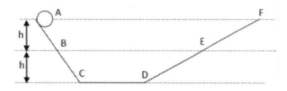

A ball is released from point A and rolls on the inclined plane given above. If there is friction only between the points D and E, which of the following about the ball is not true?

A) It can rise up to F.
B) It can never go back to A.
C) Potential energy of the ball at B is equal to the potential energy of the ball at E.
D) Kinetic energy of the ball at C is equal to the kinetic energy of the ball at D.

47

A ball is thrown vertically up with a velocity of 40 m/s. What will be the speed of the ball after 6 seconds?

A) 20 m/s pointing down
B) 20 m/s pointing up
C) 100 m/s pointing down
D) 100 m/s pointing up

48

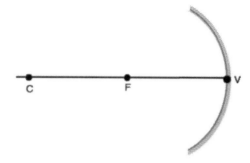

Which of the following about the reflection on a concave mirror is not correct?

A) Rays that come in parallel to the principal axis go out through the focal point.
B) Rays that come in through the focal point go out parallel to the principal axis.
C) Rays that come in through the center of curvature go out along the same path.
D) Rays that come in through the vertex go out parallel to the principal axis.

49

If the distance between two point particles is doubled, then how does the force of gravitational attraction between them change?

A) It decreases by a factor of 4.
B) It decreases by a factor of 2.
C) It increases by a factor of 2.
D) It increases by a factor of 4.

50

An object falls from a building and it takes 5 seconds for the object to reach the ground. Which of the following about this free fall is not correct? (Ignore air resistance, g= 10m/s²)

A) After three seconds, the ball's speed will be 30 m/s.
B) The mechanical energy of the ball will be conserved.
C) When the ball hits the ground its speed will be 40 m/s.
D) Kinetic energy of the ball will increase, potential energy of the ball will decrease.

51

In physics, acceleration is the rate of change of velocity of an object with respect to time.

Which of the following about acceleration is not correct?

A) The SI unit for acceleration is meter per second squared.
B) Because acceleration has both a magnitude and a direction, it is a vector quantity.
C) According to Newton's first law, when a force is applied to an object, its acceleration is inversely proportional to its mass.
D) According to Newton's second law, the acceleration of the object is directly proportional to the net force.

52

The skydiver of 50kg opens her parachute. The force due to air resistance is now 100 N. What is the acceleration of the skydiver? (g=10N/kg)

A) 2 N/kg
B) 5 N/kg
C) 8 N/kg
D) 12 N/kg

53

If the horn of the car which is moving right is honking nonstop with a frequency of 400 Hz, which of the following can be the frequencies perceived by John and Sera?

A) John; 400 Hz, Sera; 400 Hz
B) John; 380 Hz, Sera; 380 Hz
C) John; 410 Hz, Sera; 395 Hz
D) John; 364 Hz, Sera; 440 Hz

54

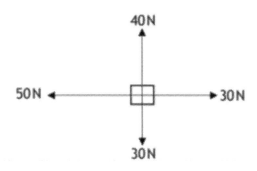

Four forces apply to an object as it is given above. What is the direction of the net force?

A) North-west
B) North of west
C) West of north
D) North-east

55

The electrical resistance of a wire is defined as the ratio of the voltage to the electric current which flows through the resistor.

Which of the following about the resistance is not correct?

A) The higher the resistance the higher the current in a circuit.
B) The resistance depends on the type, thickness and length of the wire.
C) The electrical resistance of an object is a measure of its opposition to the flow of electric current.
D) Ohm's Law states that the current in a circuit is directly proportional to the voltage across the circuit, and inversely proportional to the resistance of the circuit.

56

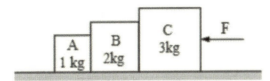

If the blocks A, B, and C are pushed by a force of 120N on a frictionless surface, what are the contact forces between the blocks?

A) Contact force between A and B is 60N, contact force between B and C is 40N.
B) Contact force between A and B is 120N, contact force between B and C is 120N.
C) Contact force between A and B is 40N, contact force between B and C is 60N.
D) Contact force between A and B is 20N, contact force between B and C is 60N.

57

Which of the following phase changes involves an increase in entropy?

A) Melting of ice
B) Dew formation
C) Frost formation
D) Freezing of water

58

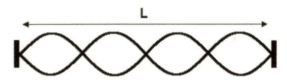

A stretched string of length 10 m vibrates at a frequency of 40 Hz producing a standing wave pattern with 4 loops. How many meters per second is the speed of the wave?

A) 8
B) 40
C) 50
D) 200

59

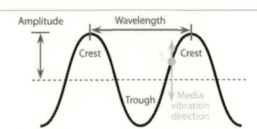

If a water wave vibrates up and down two times each second and the distance between two successive wave crests is 1.5 m, what is the speed of the wave?

A) 0.75 m/s
B) 1.5 m/s
C) 2 m/s
D) 3 m/s

60

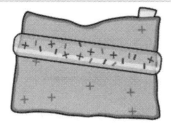

Friction can be used to create a static charge because friction between the materials causes electrons to be transferred from one material to another. If an insulator is rubbed with a cloth, it can become charged.

Which of the following about charging cloth and insulator by friction is not correct?

A) The cloth and the insulator will be oppositely charged.
B) After charging by friction cloth and insulator can repel each other.
C) If the electrons move from the insulator to the cloth, the cloth ends up with an overall negative charge.
D) If the electrons move from the cloth to the insulator, the insulator ends up with an overall negative charge.

61

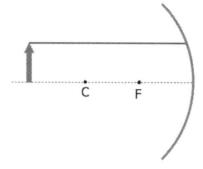

A ray from the tip of the object is sent to a concave mirror parallel to the principal axis. How will it be reflected?

A) Reflected ray will pass from the center.
B) Reflected ray will pass from the focal point.
C) Reflected ray will pass between the focal point and the vertex.
D) Reflected ray will pass between the focal point and the center.

62

A car is dripping of oil from its engine. Which of the following patterns represents the spacing of oil drops of the car that has the greatest positive acceleration?

A) • • • • • •
B) • • • • •
C) • • • • • •
D) • • • • •

63

A ball is thrown vertically up with a velocity of 40 m/s. What is the maximum height of the ball if you ignore air friction and assume gravitational acceleration, g, is 10 m/s^2?

A) 10 m
B) 20 m
C) 40 m
D) 80 m

64

Angie walks 140 feet East, and 60 feet West in 10 seconds. What is the distance and displacement of Angie?

A) Distance is 80 m, displacement is 200 m
B) Distance is 200 m, displacement is 80 m
C) Distance is 200 m, displacement is 60 m
D) Distance is 80 m, displacement is 60 m

65

If all of the forces acting on an object are balanced so that the net force is zero, then which of the following is true?

A) The object must be at rest.
B) The object's acceleration must be zero.
C) The object's average speed must be zero.
D) The object must be moving with a constant velocity.

66

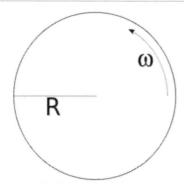

If the frequency of the rotating disc given above is 0.20 Hertz, which of the following is not true?

A) Its angular speed is 0.40π
B) Its period is 5 seconds.
C) It is rotating with 12 rpm.
D) It completes 5 rotations in one second.

67

$$R = \rho \frac{l}{A}$$

The resistance of a piece of wire depends on three factors; the length of the wire, the cross-sectional area of the wire, and the resistivity of the material composing the wire.

In which of the following conditions the resistance of a wire increases?

A) When cross-sectional area and the length decreases
B) When the cross-sectional area decreases and the length increases
C) When the cross-sectional area increases and the length decreases
D) When the cross-sectional area and the length increases

68

When the speed of an object is doubled, how does its momentum change?

A) It decreases.
B) It doubles.
C) It quadruples.
D) It remains unchanged.

69

3kg mass rotates with 4m/s around a circular path of radius of 2m. What is the centripetal force?

A) 4 N
B) 16 N
C) 24 N
D) 256 N

70

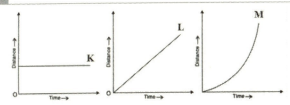

Distance-time graph of the moving objects K, L, and M are given above. According to the graphs, which of the following about the moving objects is not correct?

A) K is moving with constant speed.
B) L is moving with constant speed.
C) Speed of M is increasing.
D) L has no acceleration.

71

A force of 300 N is applied to a 60 kg object parallel to the ground. If there is 120 N friction between the object and the ground, what is the acceleration of the object?

A) 2 N/kg
B) 3 N/kg
C) 5 N/kg
D) 7 N/kg

72

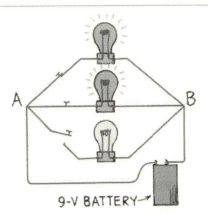

In the circuit given above each lamp has a resistor of 6 ohm and the battery has a voltage of 9 V. If the open switch is closed, what is the total (equivalent) resistor of the circuit and the current in the main branch of the circuit?

A) Total resistor 18 ohm, current 2A
B) Total resistor 18 ohm, current 0.5A
C) Total resistor 2 ohm, current 4.5A
D) Total resistor 2 ohm, current 18A

73

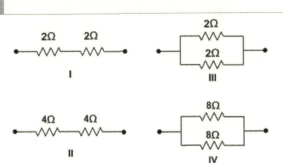

Which two arrangements of resistors given above have the same resistance between the terminals?

A) I and II
B) I and III
C) I and IV
D) III and IV

74

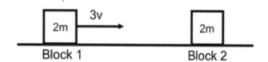

In the figure given above, Block 1 moves to the right at a speed of 3v and makes a perfect inelastic collision with Block 2 which is initially at rest.

What is the common velocity of the blocks after the collision if both of them stick and move together?

A) 1.5 v
B) 2 v
C) 3 v
D) 4 v

75

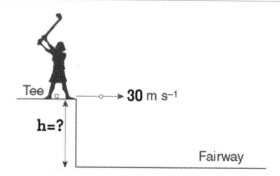

A golfer practicing on a range with an elevated tee h meter above the fairway is able to strike a ball so that it leaves the club with a horizontal velocity of 30 m/s, and hits the ground after 4s.

Which of the following about the motion of the ball is not correct? ($g = 10 m/s^2$)

A) Height of the tee is 80m.
B) Range of the ball is 120m.
C) Velocity of the ball when it hits the ground is 30 m/s.
D) Vertical velocity of the ball when it hits the ground is 40 m/s.

76

Which of the following types of electromagnetic waves has the lowest frequency?

A) Radio waves
B) Microwaves
C) Gamma waves
D) Ultraviolet waves

77

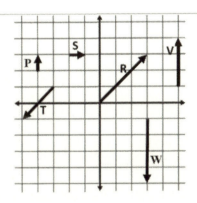

According to the vectors given above, which of the following vector additions is not correct?

A) 3P + 3S = R
B) 2S - 2P = T
C) W + V = -P
D) R + T = S + P

78

An electric motor can lift a load of 50 kg to a height of 5m at a constant speed in 4s. What is the power of the electric motor?
(g = 10 N/kg)

A) 62.5 watt
B) 250 watt
C) 625 watt
D) 2,500 watt

79

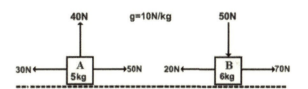

Free Body Diagram shows all the forces acting on an object and helps add them up.

Forces acting on the blocks of A and B having masses of 5kg and 6kg are shown in the figure above. What are the normal forces acting on each block?

A) Normal force acting on block A is 50N, normal force acting on block B is 60N.
B) Normal force acting on block A is 40N, normal force acting on block B is 50N.
C) Normal force acting on block A is 90N, normal force acting on block B is 10N.
D) Normal force acting on block A is 10N, normal force acting on block B is 110N.

80

In the figure given above, a girl is pushing a block, an apple is pulling the block and there is also friction between the block and the ground. If you are asked to draw the free body diagram of the block, how many different forces acting on the blok will you draw in the free body diagram?

A) 2
B) 3
C) 4
D) 5

81

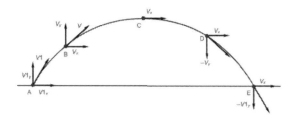

A projectile is launched at an angle of 35 degrees above the horizontal. Neglecting air resistance, what are the projectile's horizontal and vertical accelerations when it reaches its maximum height?

A) Both the horizontal and vertical accelerations are zero.
B) Both the horizontal and vertical accelerations are 9.81 N/kg.
C) The vertical acceleration is zero and the horizontal acceleration is -9.81 N/kg.
D) The vertical acceleration is -9.81 N/kg and the horizontal acceleration is zero.

82

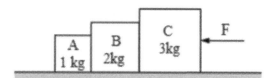

The blocks given above are initially at rest on a frictionless surface. What force should be applied on block C so that the three blocks will accelerate with 3m/s²?

A) 3 N
B) 6 N
C) 9 N
D) 18 N

83

A 6-kg fish swallows a 2-kg fish that is at rest. If the larger fish swims at 4 m/s, what is its velocity immediately after it eats the small fish?

A) 0 m/s
B) 2 m/s
C) 3 m/s
D) 4 m/s

84

A ball is dropped off a cliff and hits the ground with a velocity of 60 m/s. How high was the cliff? ($g= 10m/s^2$)

A) 6 m
B) 36 m
C) 60 m
D) 180 m

85

When two forces of 4N and 7 N are added, which of the following cannot be the resultant force?

A) 2 N
B) 4 N
C) 5 N
D) 10 N

86

A ball is thrown at an angle of 40 degrees to the horizontal.

What happens to the magnitude of the ball's vertical velocity during the time interval that the ball is in the air?

A) It decreases, then increases.
B) It increases, then decreases.
C) It remains the same.
D) It increases, then remains the same.

SECTION 6 - PHYSICS

#	Answer	Topic	Subtopic	#	Answer	Topic	Subtopic	#	Answer	Topic	Subtopic	#	Answer	Topic	Subtopic
1	A	TA	S4	23	B	TA	S4	45	A	TA	S2	67	B	TA	S2
2	D	TA	S6	24	D	TA	S3	46	A	TA	S3	68	B	TA	S8
3	C	TA	S4	25	A	TA	S5	47	A	TA	S5	69	C	TA	S6
4	C	TA	S3	26	B	TA	S6	48	D	TA	S9	70	A	TA	S5
5	D	TA	S1	27	B	TA	S2	49	A	TA	S6	71	B	TA	S6
6	D	TA	S5	28	C	TA	S4	50	C	TA	S5	72	C	TA	S2
7	C	TA	S3	29	A	TA	S6	51	C	TA	S6	73	C	TA	S2
8	B	TA	S3	30	B	TA	S6	52	C	TA	S6	74	A	TA	S8
9	D	TA	S6	31	D	TA	S3	53	D	TA	S4	75	C	TA	S5
10	A	TA	S5	32	C	TA	S5	54	B	TA	S6	76	A	TA	S4
11	B	TA	S8	33	B	TA	S5	55	A	TA	S2	77	B	TA	S5
12	C	TA	S2	34	B	TA	S5	56	D	TA	S6	78	C	TA	S3
13	D	TA	S7	35	D	TA	S5	57	A	TA	S7	79	D	TA	S6
14	C	TA	S4	36	D	TA	S6	58	D	TA	S4	80	D	TA	S6
15	C	TA	S5	37	B	TA	S6	59	D	TA	S4	81	D	TA	S5
16	C	TA	S6	38	D	TA	S5	60	B	TA	S2	82	D	TA	S6
17	A	TA	S4	39	C	TA	S4	61	B	TA	S9	83	C	TA	S8
18	A	TA	S2	40	A	TA	S6	62	C	TA	S5	84	D	TA	S5
19	D	TA	S2	41	C	TA	S3	63	D	TA	S3	85	A	TA	S6
20	B	TA	S5	42	D	TA	S2	64	B	TA	S5	86	A	TA	S5
21	D	TA	S8	43	C	TA	S3	65	B	TA	S6				
22	A	TA	S6	44	D	TA	S2	66	D	TA	S6				

Topics & Subtopics

Code	Description
SA1	MECHANICS
SA2	ELECTRICITY
SA3	WORK & ENERGY
SA4	WAVES
SA5	KINEMATICS

Code	Description
SA6	DYNAMICS
SA7	HEAT & THERMODYNAMICS
SA8	LINEAR MOMENTUM & COLLISIONS
SA9	OPTICS
TA	PHYSICS

Made in the USA
Columbia, SC
30 September 2020